Our
NOT-QUITE-HOLY
Family

"Mark and Melanie Hart have been like a brother and sister to me and my husband, offering us friendship, wisdom, and reminders to be patient as we've navigated the first few years of marriage and parenthood. This book is a perfect snapshot of the sage advice they've given to us and is absolutely essential reading for couples trying to figure out how to thrive as man and wife while inhabiting their roles as mom and dad. With easy humor, beautiful vulnerability, joyful enthusiasm, and brutal honesty, the Harts have given us all a gift in this book, and I wish it had been around when our first child was born. I'm so glad that it is here for our second."

Katie Prejean McGrady
Host of the *Ave Explores* podcast and author of *Follow*

"This book is terrific! While I may not be raising a family of my own, I definitely come into contact with many couples and families who are trying their best to love each other well and get each other to heaven. Mark and Melanie Hart's book is a gift not only for those who find themselves trying and failing but also for those who have hit their stride and are looking for people to run with. Full of practical counsel and humor, Mark and Melanie Hart have written a winner for Catholic parents (and the priests who want to help them)!"

Fr. Mike Schmitz
Director of Youth and Young Adult Ministries
Diocese of Duluth

"Is stepping on a LEGO redemptive suffering? Mark and Melanie Hart have written a treasure map for harried parents searching for honest, faithful, fun parenting. This book is a godsend. It is honest, boots-on-the-ground living in a Spirit-filled family."

Tom Wilson
Actor, writer, and comedian

"What I may like most about Mark and Melanie Hart is that they genuinely admit their faith, hope, and love in the midst of life's struggles. They don't have it all together. But they're together. So with God's help, they're on their way to becoming a holy family and are willing to help the rest of us along the way."

Lino Rulli
Host of *The Catholic Guy Show* on SiriusXM Radio

"Mark and Melanie Hart are the breath of fresh air that modern Catholic parents need. They have the wisdom of people who truly understand their faith, yet they're willing to delve into topics that you normally only whisper about with close friends after a couple of beers. Modern Catholic parenting is messy and often hard, but the Harts remind us on every page that it's possible."

Jennifer Fulwiler
Author of *Something Other Than God*

Our NOT-QUITE-HOLY Family

A Practical Guide for Catholic Parents

Mark and Melanie Hart

AVE MARIA PRESS AVE Notre Dame, Indiana

Founded in 1865, Ave Maria Press is a ministry of the United States Province of Holy Cross.

www.avemariapress.com

Paperback: ISBN-13 978-1-59471-917-2

E-book: ISBN-13 978-1-59471-918-9

Cover image © Dan Burton / Unsplash.

Cover and text design by Andy Wagoner.

Printed and bound in the United States of America.

Library of Congress Cataloging-in-Publication Data
Names: Hart, Mark, 1973- author. | Hart, Melanie, 1975- author.
Title: Our not-quite-holy family : a practical guide for Catholic parents / Mark and Melanie Hart.
Description: Notre Dame, Indiana : Ave Maria Press, 2021. | Summary: "Mark and Melanie Hart offer sincere and down-to-earth wisdom for Catholic parents, including resources and activities, to improve family life"-- Provided by publisher.
Identifiers: LCCN 2020038840 (print) | LCCN 2020038841 (ebook) | ISBN 9781594719172 (paperback) | ISBN 9781594719189 (ebook)
Subjects: LCSH: Families--Religious aspects--Catholic Church. | Families--Religious life. | Parenting--Religious aspects--Catholic Church. | Child rearing--Religious aspects--Catholic Church.
Classification: LCC BX2351 .H65 2021 (print) | LCC BX2351 (ebook) | DDC 248.4/82--dc23
LC record available at https://lccn.loc.gov/2020038840
LC ebook record available at https://lccn.loc.gov/2020038841

To Our Parents

Thank you for your love and support throughout our lives. Thank you for your hard work, your countless sacrifices—both seen and unseen—and your willingness to go without so that we never had to. We are blessed beyond measure. Thank you for your witness to marriage, for raising us in the faith, and for walking with us as we have navigated our own marriage and raised a family of our own. We love you!

Contents

Introduction

Slowly, she lowered her beautiful naked body into the bathtub.
You weren't expecting a "Catholic parenting book" to begin with that sentence, were you? Well, this isn't your typical Catholic parenting book, so keep reading. . . .

At almost nine months pregnant, stepping into that porcelain bath was a slow process. As she descended into the bubbles, trying to escape the hyperactivity of adolescent insanity on the other side of the bedroom door, she began to cry.

Not because of regret. We were excited about another child. Not because of discomfort, though it was evident. Not, even, because of time, as she had a long month still to go. No, she began to cry because, as my gorgeous bride sat down in what should have been a relaxing bath, she caught sight of a dozen naked Barbie dolls flanking the tub and staring back at her "increasingly disproportionate" body (her words, not mine). If I could have bought her a Malibu Dreamhouse in that moment, I would have.

"I'm retaining more water than a dam," Melanie said with a sincere yet uncomfortable smile.

Melanie was thirty-five weeks pregnant with more than a month to go, and it was an abnormally long summer even by Arizona standards. Our entire family was penned up together on a 115-degree desert summer day, and our older children were going stir-crazy inside.

There was little, as her husband, that I could do to ease her discomfort. Back and foot rubs, though soothing, can only take an expectant mother so far. I found myself praying in desperation that the Lord would give her some relief. And, quite honestly, I was praying in gratitude that I was a man.

I'm not sure why God in his infinite wisdom decided that women would conceive, nurture, and carry babies, but I, for one, am grateful. If men were the ones called to have children, the human race might die out. Incidentally, it also makes one wonder what the male seahorse must have done wrong that God designed him to carry the babies rather than the female . . . but let's not digress.

Pregnancy, although wild, is just the preview—the sneak peek, if you will—of the joy and pain, the magic and madness, of parenthood. It foreshadows and prepares a couple for the unfathomable journey that lies before them.

Childbirth Is Hard . . . on the Man?

Nothing can ready you, as a couple, for your first pregnancy or experience of childbirth. You can read all the books and take all the classes. Those things help, but nothing can properly prepare someone for all that childbirth (and childrearing) brings with it.

Whether the birth occurs in a hospital or at home, naturally or with an epidural, *everyone has a story*, and every story is unique. In the end, the entire experience is like a beautiful car accident: there is terror and noise, screaming and fluids (oh, so many fluids), trained medical professionals, possibly some scarring, and your life is forever different afterward. Obviously, we jest . . . sort of.

Sitting in the delivery room with Melanie as she prepared to give birth to our first child, I was "ready." The camera batteries were charged. Priest friends across multiple time zones were offering up their daily Mass intention for our family. Cloisters of nun friends were on their knees rollin' those rosary beads. One of the blessings of working in ministry for so many years is that you amass a lot of friends and acquaintances who are obliged to pray for you when you ask. And oh, I needed those prayers that day.

I had mastered the breathing rhythms. I watched the fetal monitor with the precision and attention of a sentry in a tower. I fed my uncomfortable bride her ice chips and communicated with family waiting outside. I had the template for the first baby picture and birth announcement already set up on my Walgreens account, ready to print out the first photo my bride approved moments after our daughter arrived. In short, I was on pace for "Father of the Year" honors.

I held Melanie's hand as she began to push, affirming, breathing, comforting. As my wife reminded me several times, I "was the reason" we were in this position (well, me, and a very romantic dinner forty weeks prior, but let's not split hairs). Melanie pushed for what felt like an eternity, as I hunched over her bed holding her tiny yet impressively strong hand. As the hormones raged and the adrenaline surged, I wondered if I'd ever have full blood flow (or dexterity) in that hand again. Actually, as every bone and tendon in my body ached, I silently prayed for relief and briefly considered asking the otherwise-busy doctor for medical attention. (Do OBs work on hands?)

At any rate, it was showtime. The head crowned. The long-awaited moment was upon us. Everything went quickly. Our daughter shot out like a bobsled. Wailing, laughing, crying, it was like a family holiday dinner but with fewer people and less clothing. Melanie allowed me to video the birth, and perhaps only male readers will appreciate this . . . even with all the drama, I never once lost focus or let the action fall out of frame. Silent fist bump!

When I put the camera down and cut the cord, the nurses rushed our daughter off to be weighed and cleaned up. I finally stood up straight and without thinking uttered aloud, "Ugh, wow . . . my back hurts."

~☆~

Little did we understand, as a couple, how parenthood would magnify everything.

∽

At that moment I realized I was the only man in the room. I'd never wished so badly that I could take a sentence back or that I owned a DeLorean that could travel back in time. I realized how my exclamation must have seemed heartless and thoughtless to the human who just *squeezed* a human out of her body. Afraid to look at my exhausted bride, I instead gazed down to her female OB at the foot of the bed, who looked at me in silent disbelief and began shaking her head as if to say, "Mark, you're an idiot."

When I finally did lock eyes with Melanie, she grinned and simply said, "Oh, really?" but implied, "You're going to pay for that." Luckily for me, she has an incredible sense of humor, even in stressful moments.

Little did I, as a father, understand the journey that we had just embarked on. Little did Melanie, as a mother, comprehend how physically and emotionally exhausting that journey would be each day and each season of life.

Little did we understand, as a couple, how parenthood would magnify everything.

When you get married in the Church and unleash the grace of the Sacrament of Matrimony, everything gets revealed: your blessings and your sins, your gifts and your pride, your hopes and your shame. The sacrament improves everything that's right and exposes everything that's wrong. Then, if the Lord sends you children, it all gets magnified again. With children, everything right in the relationship gets even better . . . and everything still wrong gets even harder. The new life of a child brings with it the opportunity for new death to self and sacrifice, daily.

Dying for a Living

Parenthood does so many things. It reveals depths of love within you that you never knew existed. It calls you to levels of self-sacrifice that seem almost heroic. Parenthood is how God blesses you out of your selfishness and floods your soul with love, all while reminding you how little you really know and how desperately you need his grace and help.

Little did we understand that parenthood was also going to consist of a series of desired do-over moments. We obviously aren't perfect, not even close. We don't claim to be. We are human and fallen. Our love is often conditional and fickle. We would like to offer glory story after glory story on the pages that follow, but what we will offer here instead is a series of falls and fails and what we are learning along the way.

We are not child psychologists. We are not marriage counselors. We are not even very good Catholics, at least not compared to all the seemingly perfect Catholic families we worship next to or exchange Christmas cards with. We are trying to be holy, but we're not quite there yet. (Hence, the reason for this book's title.)

In fact, we are probably more accurately described as "bad Catholics" who are messy and sinful, but who are also passionate and transparent. We are not parents who assume our kids are perfect and do nothing wrong. Those parents are quite annoying, especially at school functions. A fifteen-minute conversation with them surely takes at least a year off of purgatory. (The previous sentence has no theological backing . . . but we stand by it.)

No, we are the parents usually showing up late to Mass with our kids in tow. We're the ones who—when the school calls—assume guilt of our kids before innocence, not because they're bad, but because we are constantly aware of the fact that we need to do better.

So, why in the world are *we* writing this book? Well, there are three reasons, primarily:

1. We acknowledge our sinfulness and need for God's mercy, every day. We are a mess, but we admit it and want to share how this knowledge has changed our marriage and parenting for the better.

2. We have learned many lessons and gained important insight while raising kids from elementary school all the way into college. We have the battle scars to prove it and are sure you can relate to some of our experiences as well.

3. We have learned that to grow as parents we need to deal with practical realities instead of theoretical ideas. There are plenty of parenting books written with ideas that are untested, unproven, or one-size-fits-all. This book serves to uphold the truth that every family—like every marriage—is intensely unique. If Old Navy teaches us anything, it's that one size does not fit all . . . one size fits none. We know this, we respect this reality, and we want to share in this journey with you.

If Old Navy teaches us anything, it's that one size does not fit all . . . one size fits none.

On the pages that follow, we look at various facets and strategies of parenting, from protecting your relationship as a couple to protecting your children from themselves and the culture around them. We tackle faulty parenting assumptions, "logical" parenting approaches that bear little fruit, and practical tools for fostering faith in your children in a way that won't cause resentment as they get older. We discuss the struggles of everything from "screen time" to the need for family time to sibling drama and a lot of stuff in between that almost every modern family is forced to deal with, too.

We'll share successes and failures we've experienced firsthand over the past twenty years. We'll share ideas, tips, pitfalls, strategies, stories, verses, quotes, and prayers from us, from the Bible, and from our Catholic tradition. We've included an appendix with helpful prayers and another appendix with stories and advice from an array of amazing Catholic parents, all with one hope: *to help you get your spouse and kids to heaven.*

That's the goal.

In his first letter, our first pope, St. Peter, simply and succinctly outlined our goal as parents and as Christians: "The goal of [your] faith, the salvation of your souls" (1 Pt 1:9). Notice that the verse doesn't say "the salvation of your soul," but, rather, "souls." The inference and expectation is that our faith will lead souls (plural) to salvation, the first of which are the ones living and growing and learning in the domestic church we call home.

So, whether you're a parent-to-be, an exhausted new parent, a parent of little ones in elementary school, a parent of hormonally hyperactive middle or high schoolers, a parent sending off your kids to the best atheist college professors money can buy, or a parent/grandparent trying to "keep" your kids or grandkids Catholic, happy, and safe in this increasingly crazy world, this book is for you. Hell, it's for all of us, because we're all in this thing together.

Before you turn this page, though, let us pose one final question: How far are you willing to go for your family to see heaven? Stop and consider this question, prayerfully, for a moment.

How far are you willing to go for your family to see heaven?

Would you say you've done everything you can until this point to guide your spouse and kids to the Lord? Are you willing to be uncomfortable if it means that your family will, ultimately, be happier? Is there anything you wouldn't do to save your child's life? How about their soul?

Parenthood isn't for the weak of heart. It's an invitation from the Lord to unleash the hidden greatness of your soul. He would not have entrusted young souls to you if he didn't believe in your ability to lead them to him. God believes far more in you than you do in him or in yourself.

Trust his judgment. Turn this page. Let's have some fun.

1

Pros Don't Raise Cons

———————————————➤

Proactive Parenting versus Reactive Parenting

It was supposed to be a happy day. Well, maybe not happy—
it was Ash Wednesday, after all—but it wasn't supposed to
start out like it did.

We rushed out the door to get our kids to Mass and
school. Our youngest daughter was about four years old at
the time, and to call her a girly-girl would be an understatement. She's our sassiest child, to be sure. Once, during her
elementary-school years, when we asked her if she'd want
to consider becoming a nun, her response was, "Can nuns
wear high heels?"

We're still holding out hope that if anyone ever estab-
lishes an order called Our Lady of the Stiletto, our daughter
will reopen her discernment.

On this particular morning, we were just hoping to
make it through Mass peacefully. With three kids in tow,
we found Mass was always one part hostage negotiation
and three parts redirection. Longer Masses like the one on

Ash Wednesday posed a particular challenge in that every additional prayer only served to stretch the already-thin patience even further.

The distribution of ashes began in the usual way. The priest, deacon, and lay ministers with the ashes took their positions, and lines of parishioners formed down each aisle. Our family rose—pious as hell (how's that for an oxymoron?)—and slowly proceeded forth like the sinners we are. Our eldest two daughters received their ashes. Next up was our youngest girl—our sequin-loving, bedazzled-desiring, glitter-bomb diva. As the deacon extended his hand to mark her with the charred outward sign of Catholic penitence, our daughter quickly dodged his soot-covered thumb like she was competing in the World Dodgeball Championship. When he tried again to apply the ashes, our daughter became almost ninja-like in her reflexes.

We were both embarrassed and growing in frustration. And then, when we thought it could not get more humiliating, it happened. Our little angel—the apple of our eye—turned into a holy terror for all the parish to see. In a reaction that can only be described as quasi-liturgical self-defense, she swept her arm up, making contact with the bowl of ashes in the deacon's hand and sending it flying. The bowl soared easily twelve feet in the air before crashing down on the altar steps and discharging a cloud of dust that covered a quarter of the sanctuary.

We stood in shocked disbelief, still waiting to receive the sinner's mark that we both obviously deserved for raising such a seemingly unholy child. Like any good deacon, ours had a mustache, and said 'stache was now peppered with the ash of burnt palm fronds. We scanned the church for a rock to crawl beneath, but to no avail. There we stood, surrounded by fellow sinners bearing the mark, but the Harts . . . we had taken "not quite holy" to stunning new heights.

We had taken "not quite holy" to stunning new heights.

Of course, we'd love to say that was the only public display of shame we have suffered as parents, but that would be a straight lie.

There was the time our daughter, when asked by our pastor if she had listened to the homily, responded with a quick, "Which homily, Father? My dad always says you give three every Sunday." Luckily for us, that pastor was transferred to a new parish not long after, and we could stop hiding from him.

Then there was the time our youngest child, our son, was playing with a small car he smuggled into Mass. It fell on the ground, and he disappeared to retrieve it, or so we thought. Moments later, the car was racing toward the sanctuary. It was a pull-back-and-release-to-fly-forward type of car . . . and fly forward it did. Not only did it almost take out one of the altar servers but it also offered us the unique embarrassment of having to walk up in front of the entire congregation to retrieve it.

Then there was the parent-teacher conference where we learned that our daughter was correcting the religion teacher whenever she made a mistake telling a Bible story. (For the record, Melanie is proud to say that fault lies squarely with Mark.)

And then there was the time, when asked, "Do your parents have any hobbies?" our daughter promptly responded, "Does sitting on the couch, holding hands, and drinking wine count as a hobby?"

The list goes on. You get the idea.

Baby Steps (in the Wrong Direction?)

What a beautiful mess we are, huh? A work in progress, if you will.

During some months and seasons, we do a good job maintaining quality family time and regular prayer together, and other times, we are a spiritual train wreck. Of course, our deepest desire and hope for our kids is that they will not only love and live out their Catholic faith but, ultimately, make it to heaven. It's likely yours, too.

We learned early on with our children that intentions weren't enough. Actions follow beliefs. If we believe in God and in the importance of the faith, then it's not enough to say we are Catholic; we have to live it.

Yes, our daughter caused an ash explosion, but at least we made it to Mass—and on Ash Wednesday, which isn't even a holy day of obligation! Sure, our child unintentionally insulted our pastor's lengthy and digressive homilies, but at least she was listening (if not to him, to her father)! While our son's toy car interrupted the liturgy and embarrassed us all, at least it allowed the other—far better—parents in the pews that day to exit feeling affirmed and more confident about their own child-rearing! Yes, our child disrespectfully corrected her teacher's flawed biblical recounts and miniheresies, but at least she had learned the stories well enough to notice the errors. She believed that her classmates deserved the correct version of sacred writ. And, yes, our daughter made us sound like full-blown alcoholics with her wine comment, but at least she got to see her parents cuddling up and enjoying time together.

Actions follow beliefs.

We can obviously improve when it comes to our children's Mass behavior, their interpersonal communication skills (or lack thereof), and our ongoing witness to them, but none of these embarrassing moments would have occurred if we weren't proactively trying to introduce them to the faith at church, at home, and at school.

Think of it this way. If you are sitting in a car, is it easier to turn the wheels if the car is moving or parked? The answer is when the car is in motion, of course. When you sit in a parked car on a driveway, it can be really tough to turn the wheels. When the car is moving, though—even in the wrong direction—it's a lot easier. You may be barreling down a road in the way opposite of your deepest hopes and intentions, but at least you're moving and not stagnant! That's why no matter how successful you have or haven't been with your parenting, especially in regard to handing on the faith, there is always hope.

Right about now, some of you may be feeling really good about yourselves because your children are so well behaved, and God bless you for it! Well done. Others of you might be feeling better because your parenting doesn't seem so bad in comparison. And then, a few of you may be identifying with us, saying, "We can relate." Lastly, those souls praying for or currently awaiting children are wondering what the secret is to never having these situations arise.

The Million-Dollar Answer

"Wait until your father gets home!" was a frequently uttered threat in Mark's childhood. It could be translated to mean, "You've got about another two hours of freedom before you meet your Maker."

Now that we are parents, we recognize that when Mark's mother made this sort of comment, she was likely feeling overwhelmed and was *reacting* to specific situations. Reacting without thinking is understandable. Who among us hasn't flipped out on our kids occasionally? We admit that we don't always step back to gather our composure and remember that we love our kids before responding in stressful situations. We are certainly guilty of this, but we're constantly trying to practice *proactive* instead of *reactive* parenting.

Consider these classic scenarios that often give rise to a reaction in a parent:

- Your child's room is a mess with clothes all over the floor.

- Your child dings the car for the first time or gets their first speeding ticket.

- Your child doesn't study and fails a test.

- Your child misses curfew.

- Your child stares at their screen rather than making eye contact and listening to you.

- Your child deliberately disobeys when you ask them to stop doing x or y.

- Your child rolls their eyes when you are correcting them.

- Your child lies to you about something, and you catch them in the lie.

- Your child talks back to you with disrespect.

These common moments of preadolescent or adolescent life often stir a reaction in parents, no matter how patient they are. It's normal. It's human. Reactions, however, rarely yield the results we desire. Rather than defusing the situation, reacting tends to pour kerosene on the fire. Now the child in question feels not only ashamed but also attacked.

Rather than defusing the situation, reacting tends to pour kerosene on the fire.

So, what is the secret to raising "good" kids, or getting kids to like Mass, or developing kids who want to stay in the Catholic faith? What's the million-dollar answer?

The secret is that there is no secret. There is no easy, one-size-fits-all, magic-bullet answer to the question. *It's all about being proactive and taking each situation one at a time.* To extend the million-dollar question, it's as if God is placing a challenge before you as a parent.

Let's say that getting your children to heaven is going to cost you one million dollars and that, just for argument's sake, you actually had the million dollars. God would say to you, "It's going to cost you the million dollars, but I don't want you to write me a check. I want you to pay it out one dollar at a time, multiple times a day." Put simply, every moment we as parents choose patience or breathe peace rather than reacting in annoyance or anger, we are paying out one dollar.

If we have the ears of heaven, we can almost hear the money transfer one bill at a time. Your child's room is always a mess, and instead of yelling, you calmly sit down with them (preferably not in the pigsty they call a room), explain why it's important to take care of their belongings, and discuss both expectations and consequences moving forward. Right there is one dollar toward the million.

The key in these moments is to remember that whatever the situation . . . it's not about you. You have been given these children—these adolescents—to direct and form and guide. Don't take any situation personally, even if your kids lean toward language or behavior you find disrespectful or thoughtless.

❧

The key in these moments is
to remember that whatever
the situation . . . it's not about you.

☙

Often as parents, if our child disobeys, breaks the rules, or goes against our will, we take it personally. The thing is, though, that it's not personal. They're kids. When they're emotional or lazy or sassy, you might want to react, but that won't change their behavior and it won't teach them anything. They're not doing anything *to* you. They merely did something wrong. They broke a rule; they pushed a boundary. Where parents go wrong is to focus more than on their personal feelings of annoyance or disrespect than on the child's development.

If your child walks in late for curfew or brings in their first speeding ticket, rather than flying into a rage regarding their irresponsibility or the unnecessary worry they've caused, call them out for it (calmly) and ask them to wait in another room to talk about their consequence. Before you decide on the consequence, say a prayer of thanksgiving that they are okay. Then pray a Hail Mary to calm your heart before discussing the consequence. Once you have set and communicated the punishment—the phone or keys taken, for instance—engage in a stern yet loving conversation that reaffirms your great love for them and desire for their ultimate safety. You'll also need to talk about what happens when trust is broken. You can almost hear a twenty-dollar bill getting transferred from your account on that one.

When a child talks back, it can be infuriating. Practically speaking, however, we need to ask ourselves, "Why are they talking back?" and "If I lose my temper and raise my voice, is it really going to help the situation or just make it worse?" Perhaps when we ask a normal question, they quickly get defensive. How can we parent them in a way that focuses on and reveals why they are getting defensive, rather than devolving into an argument of he said/she said? Where is that defensiveness coming from? Is it, perhaps, the reaction we model as parents? Did Mom or Dad come across in an accusatory or attacking way? Did we get too emotionally involved, and now they are simply mirroring what they witnessed in us?

The most important thing we can do in parenting—above everything else—is to respect our children. It is the foundation for everything. Simply put, if we don't respect our children, they will not respect us. "Do as I say, not as I do" is not only an antiquated and philosophically poor approach; it's also hypocritical and often outright scarring.

This is what St. Paul was speaking about when he told parents to love each other and their kids and not to provoke one another to anger (see Ephesians 6:1–4, Colossians 3:18–21, and 1 Thessalonians 2:10–12). Surely he knew that parents love their children, but he also knew that in our humanity there are times that it *does not come across to them that we do.*

Remember the old cliché: You are the thermostat (as the parents) and not the thermometer. You are the ones who should set the temperature and tone, not merely reflect it. Every time we, as parents, are proactive in our communication rather than reactive in our frustration, heaven applauds. Stop now and consider the past few weeks with your own children. Picture the moments that upset or frustrated you the most. How did you handle and express that frustration? Did your child walk away understanding why you were upset? At any time did they question your love for them? Do they "know" that you love them but possibly think you don't "like" them? In retrospect, how could you have parented better in those situations?

Every time we, as parents, are proactive in our communication rather than reactive in our frustration, heaven applauds.

They say hindsight is 20/20, but, in reality, love sees 20/20. Love sees the soul and not just the action. Love desires mercy, not just sacrifice. Love elicits understanding, not just obedience. Love is shown not merely in the words we use but also in the expressions we display, the respect we offer, and the tone they hear. When we love, we are seeing our kids—the most precious gifts that God the Father has *entrusted to* us (see James 1:17)—with 20/20 vision. Parenthood gives us the opportunity both to see as God the Father sees and to love as God the Father loves.

Alexander Pope said, "To err is human; to forgive, divine." When we err (and choose to sin), we act as humans act. When we forgive, we act as God does. After thinking back through those recent situations that caused you frustration or where you could have done a better job moderating your tone or words or volume, do you see a need to *seek forgiveness* from your children, and perhaps your spouse as well, for any particular moment? Do you need to *offer forgiveness* for any particular incident? If so, what's stopping you? Pride is the only poison anyone in your family should swallow.

Moving Forward (Practical Steps)

1. Read and pray Colossians 3:12–17. Print it out and leave it on your nightstand; put it on the fridge or next to your coffee maker. Read it daily until you have it committed to memory:

   > Put on then, as God's chosen ones, holy and beloved, heartfelt compassion, kindness, humility, gentleness, and patience, bearing with one another and forgiving one another, if one has a grievance against another; as the Lord has forgiven you, so must you also do. And over all these put on love, that is, the bond of perfection. And let the peace of Christ control your hearts, the peace into which you were also called in one body. And be thankful. Let the word of Christ dwell in you richly, as in all wisdom you

teach and admonish one another, singing psalms, hymns, and spiritual songs with gratitude in your hearts to God.

And whatever you do, in word or deed, do everything in the name of the Lord Jesus, giving thanks to God the Father through him.

2. Remember the goal of your parenting is to raise well-formed young souls. If you see your spouse beginning to lose their temper in a situation, look at them and simply say, "Remember the goal." God has entrusted these souls to you for a reason. You are capable of more than you think you are with the help of his grace.

3. Read and share 1 Corinthians 13:4–8 with your kids. Learn it one verse at a time as a family:

Love is patient, love is kind. It is not jealous, is not pompous, it is not inflated, it is not rude, it does not seek its own interests, it is not quick-tempered, it does not brood over injury, it does not rejoice over wrongdoing but rejoices with the truth. It bears all things, believes all things, hopes all things, endures all things.

Love never fails.

4. Evaluate yourself daily according to these three parenting necessities: love, teach, and guide. Everything else—feeding them, washing their clothes, providing for them financially—though important, must follow (and will naturally flow from) these first three: love, teach, and guide.

5. Dads, look up Ephesians 6:4. Moms, look up Proverbs
   31:25–26. Ask yourself how well you're living this
   passage out, and then spend a few minutes in prayer.

Closing Prayer

Father in heaven, give us the patience we need on earth. Be
with us in the frustrating moments, the anxious moments,
and the stressful moments. Help us to see past the mess,
through the anger, and into the young minds and hearts
that you have entrusted to us. Grant us the wisdom we need
for their guidance and correction—to be strong but loving, firm yet fair, and convicted without convicting. Mother
Mary, teach us how to become more thoughtful and less
reactive. By your intercession, may we, like you, learn to
better ponder all things in our hearts.

2

Stuck in Reverse

———————

Dealing with Our Families of Origin

Once upon a time, I (Mark) was so desperate to demonstrate my authority over my children that I threatened to cut in half a mermaid doll that my then five- and three-year-old daughters couldn't manage to share. That's my confession, but let it be known that this was never my intention. When the war broke out among my offspring, I trotted out my usual parenting tactics: comforting ("It's okay, sweetie; take a deep breath and tell me why you're upset"), reasoning ("Let's take turns!"), bribing ("I'll give you a piece of candy if you be a big girl and let your little sister go first"), and threatening ("Do it now, or you're going to time-out!"). None of this worked, so I turned to the Bible, as I tend to do in moments of desperation.

There is a famous scene in 1 Kings 3:16–28 when King Solomon, considered the wisest man ever to live, was faced with a dilemma. Two women appeared in Solomon's court, each claiming that she was the mother of the same child. After hearing both of their stories, with each woman insisting that her own version was true, the king sent for a sword and asked his guard to divide the child in two, giving one half to each woman. When the first woman heard this command, she pleaded with the king not to harm the child but to give him to her adversary instead. Seeing her great love for the welfare of the child, the king wisely knew that she was, indeed, the real mother.

So, why not try it, right? It worked for King Solomon, so why not for me? I did what any other rational, loving parent would do when children won't share. I placed Ariel squarely on the table in front of both my daughters. I gently admonished them about the need to share and to love their sibling above any possession. Then I held the shears to the doll and waited for one of them to stop me. Neither one flinched. They just looked on curiously to see what would happen.

We didn't have a clue about how to cultivate gentler hearts in them without breaking their spirits.

Well, I couldn't follow through with such a thing in the end, and we drove to Target an hour later. Problem solved, but, more important, an underlying problem was revealed. We had different kids with very different temperaments who were also stubborn and strong-willed. And we didn't have a clue about how to cultivate gentler hearts in them without breaking their spirits. How would we teach them empathy and thoughtfulness without overzealous chastisement and reaction? How could we be the parents that our kids needed us to be? How could we overcome our own weaknesses and default emotional reactions to be receptive to the uniqueness of each child? It was a challenge neither of us was prepared for and that only one of us was capable of handling, to be honest.

Two Harts, One Mission

Before we had kids, we had vastly different parenting philosophies, and we've had to work through those differences to find out what God is calling us to and what we are actually capable of. It can be easy in today's world to compare our own lives to what we see on social media, but we aren't called to any of that. We are called to be true to the unique individuals God created us to be, and that means we will each have our own parenting style, strengths, and weaknesses. To start to grasp all of this, we've found it helpful to look back at our own families of origin to discover where our first ideas about parenting came from.

The parenting strategy that I (Mark) intended to implement was based on absolutely zero research or empirical data. I just assumed that logic and structure would solve any problem that came our way. Then, the craziest thing happened as we began to have kids: They didn't come out with the same personalities or temperaments as us! They were all individual souls with different gifts, needs, and struggles.

These unfathomable gifts entrusted to us by God were not mass-produced droids from an assembly line. Weird, right?

The truth, though I didn't understand it at the time, is that I was operating under what we call a "parental default." That is, I was subconsciously planning on doing what my parents did. I mean, I turned out okay (or so I thought), so why not?

To offer some context for my philosophy, let me mention that I came from a family of six kids (five boys). Our father was a hard-working but stern man with a thousand-yard stare that could burn a hole through you, while our mother was the heart of the home, a prayer warrior who, unbeknownst to many, had superpowers. Her gifts ranged from the ever-popular eyes in the back of her head to the even more impressive look that could induce tears of guilt or a speedy confession for any number of sins. But the skill that dwarfed the others was her linguistic prowess.

You see, my mom could turn any noun into a verb. For example, when it was dinnertime and I was playing out back, she'd call me in, demonstrating a unique command of the Queen's English.

"Ma-a-r-rk! Dinner's ready!" she would yell out the back door of our suburban Chicago home in a volume loud enough for kids in Wisconsin to hear. My natural strategy was to stall, hoping to squeeze every last second of freedom and ounce of daylight from my preadolescent utopian existence. "But, Mom," I'd call back, "I'm on the swing set!"

It was in this moment that my mother's super skill set moved into high gear as she would retort something like, "Mark Joseph, get in here now or *I'll swing-set you!*"

In moments like these—as with the use of the first *and* middle names—there was little room for misinterpretation. When a noun became a verb, your day was over, and, if you hesitated, your life was assuredly over, too.

Despite this upbringing, I lived a majority of my adolescent and adult life believing my parents were perfect. I didn't want to *become* them, as I said countless times in my teenage years, but if someone else were to suggest they were not great parents, I'd take serious offense to it. Never mind the passive aggression, unrealistic expectations, or personal woundedness that would come through in their parenting styles—that stuff didn't translate to paper.

On paper, my parents were married more than fifty years. They never missed Sunday Mass and raised six college graduates, each going on to a successful leadership position in their field of choice. Their parenting philosophy must have been bulletproof, right? Sadly, no. While I'm more thankful than words can express for my parents and for the life they gave us, I ignorantly operated according to a flawed premise of artificial success. A sort of shiny "don't ask" Christmas-card Catholicism, which never really dealt with a problem but rather tucked it safely away in the powder keg of repression for safekeeping. I knew my parents weren't perfect—none are, to be sure—but I stupidly believed that because of my siblings' academic and professional successes, my parents' approach to parenting must have been right. I thought they had it all figured out and, since we hadn't raised a Manson or a Dahmer in the family, that I would adopt the same methods. But, as I'm sure you've caught on by now, that parental default is where problems begin.

Default Mode Overload

It can be perilous to adopt the parenting tactics of your own parents without first considering how they fit with your personality and family dynamics. For example, assumptions about the division of household duties can spring from a default marriage mode (i.e., the husband does the yardwork and the wife does all the cooking; or the husband pays the bills and the wife does the laundry). Even though such expectations aren't shared as generally in the twenty-first century, they can lie subconsciously beneath the surface in a man or woman early on in marriage. These default modes of thinking hopefully emerge during dating and marriage prep, but if they are left uncommunicated, they can become a recipe for disaster—unspoken assumptions that can foster frustration and resentment that spill out when children come, sleep is in short supply, and stress levels increase.

Perhaps the marriage and parenting defaults that can be the trickiest to identify have to do with our emotional reactions. Whether you fly off the handle when your children talk back or you feel unloved when your spouse doesn't greet you with a sign of affection, seemingly small patterns of feelings and behaviors can have an enormous impact on your marriage and family. We've learned the hard way that it's best to communicate our expectations and hopes so that everyone in the family can be on the same page.

Crafting Your Family Mission Statement

It's vital for couples to have a common vision of what success looks like at home and not just view parenting as a shared workload. This is one reason we believe so strongly that every couple should have a mission statement for their marriage and family. It should be something you can craft together, live by, and, as the kids get older, introduce to your children. Every couple's mission statement will look different, but here are some priorities that you may want to consider:

- Putting your marriage relationship first.
- Incorporating your Catholic faith.
- Committing to serving others as a family.
- Practicing hospitality and having a home open to visitors.
- Making healthy lifestyle choices.
- Teaching your kids about the faith.
- Fostering prayer and virtue within the home.

It's vital for couples to have a common vision of what success looks like at home.

We recommend taking this project to prayer and asking the Lord to guide you as you write down what you hope for your marriage and family. We did this very thing seventeen years ago and came up with this mission statement:

> We will put God first in our marriage, family, and home. We will pray daily both alone and as a family. We will share our sacrament and Catholic faith with joy. Our home will be a place where the name and goodness of God are proclaimed to all who enter. We will speak the truth with love, admit our mistakes, and offer and seek forgiveness from one another. We will work to keep our minds, bodies, and souls healthy, strong, and pure. We will be grateful for our blessings and share those blessings with others. We are Harts.

Our mission statement isn't perfect by any stretch (you might even say it's not-quite-holy!), but it's enough to keep us grounded. It helps keep things in right order, and when sickness or job changes or financial stresses come, it helps ensure that we make decisions based on who we want to be (as a family) and not on default reactions or emotions.

Begin crafting your own statement by asking yourselves, "What does God desire from and for our marriage and family?" Next, move through the charisms that your family can offer extended family, friends, the Church, and society in general. Finally, consider what kind of example you want your family to be to other families and how you want to be remembered by your own kids and others.

Practicing Discernment

Beyond setting goals as a couple, if we want to be successful and faithful as parents, we must also become discerning.

The word *discernment* comes from a Latin term meaning "to separate apart." When we practice discernment, we seek to delineate between different interests. We might examine our default emotional and behavioral patterns, our long-held presumptions, and our rash judgments of others. Many times, this process involves a humble look into our history. Putting pride aside, we have to take a long, hard look at where our families of origin succeeded, came up short, and outright failed.

─❀─

Playing the blame game or becoming a martyr won't make you a better parent.

↝

Then we have to ask ourselves how all of this background noise plays out in our minds and actions today. It's important that you not get bogged down by the negative stuff. It's in the past, and while it affects your perspectives and motivations today, playing the blame game or becoming a martyr won't make you a better parent, and your spouse will probably get pretty annoyed. Instead, we suggest owning your whole story—the good and the bad. Start out by asking yourself some basic questions and, in a spirit of vulnerability, invite your spouse to weigh in. Here are a few questions to get the process started:

Ask Yourself: Families of Origin Questions

1. Have you become like your dad or mom in your parenting? If so, in what ways has it been good and in what ways bad?

2. If you haven't emulated your parents, has it been a conscious decision not to do so? Why?

3. Is there healing you need to experience regarding your own upbringing before you can bring up another person in a healthy way?

4. Do you understand that choosing not to follow your own parents' example of upbringing is not an indictment of them?

5. Do you know and believe that, just as your parents had struggles and challenges, your spouse and you have unique challenges that will inform and possibly upend your parenting?

Taking a long and hard look at your family of origin is critical if you are going to be the best parent you are called to be. Letting go of anger, cultivating empathy, tearing down false pedestals and artificial harmonies, and becoming increasingly self-aware are difficult yet productive and profound ways to change your parenting philosophy. These changes *will* redirect your family on a path to its own unique joy and peace.

I (Melanie) come from a divorced and blended family, which heavily influences my viewpoints on marriage and family life. My birth parents divorced when I was seven years old, leaving my older brother and me living mainly with my working mom. The split was not amicable and caused great stress as we went back and forth between different homes, lifestyles, and approaches to parenting. My brother and I were forced to mature emotionally quite early. Both parents remarried. My mom married a lifelong Catholic, and though raised Protestant until then, we entered the Church ourselves when I was eight. In reality, my faith didn't take root or become my own until I took part in a Life Teen program at my local parish in high school. In fact, it was Mark who first invited me to Mass with him when I was fifteen. Between my own upbringing and years spent as a nanny, I've seen the inherent risks of unilaterally adopting parenting methods—good or bad—from those who came before us.

Studying psychology, child development, and family relations during my undergrad years gave me a more holistic view of the challenges modern families face and of what healthy parenting requires. You can have all the strategies and philosophical approaches you want. You can read every parenting book, but each child is unique. There is no "one size fits all." We have to cherish and treat every child differently because God made them unique and beautiful *and different.* Sure, we can have consistent rules and standards in the household, but each situation and soul requires understanding and special attention. We can't, as parents, heap heavy expectations on kids: Let them be kids and develop at their own pace. In doing so, we both honor their individuality and offer each of them the freedom to grow into the person God designed them to be.

I (Mark) am utterly amazed by Melanie's approach. She is a master craftsman as a parent. She is patient, compassionate, and empathetic in ways I can scarcely comprehend. I learn from her every day, not because she's perfect but because she is malleable and humble. She is the first one to tell you she *doesn't have it all figured out*, and I've had to learn from her that we don't need to be perfect parents to be good-enough parents.

It takes more than childbirth to be a true parent. It takes heightened self-awareness, understanding your own wounds and sins and pains and how, if you're unwilling to deal with them, you will pass those same sins and pains along to your children. I once heard someone say, "You think and talk like those you listen to the most." If true, it's a good reminder to us parents to act and speak with self-awareness.

Why do we think that just because kids come from the same parents that they'll hold the same viewpoints and values, good or bad? Parents can raise kids in the same environment, according to the same rules and with the same traditions, and see radically different results in each child, for better or worse. We all want to raise successful kids. God wants us to raise holy kids. Success is hard enough, but holiness requires God's grace and a whole lot of prayer. Even if you and your spouse are an ideal Catholic couple, there's no guarantee your kids will pick up that mantle, because every child is different.

We each have to do the hard work of examining ourselves and our assumptions. The question boils down to: *Do you love your spouse and children enough to do battle with your own demons?* You owe it to them to work to control what you can within yourself before unknowingly passing on your unresolved issues to them later. Setting attainable goals and taking an honest look at your own upbringing are vital to becoming the parent God calls you to be. We know that our families of origin play a part in who we become. The degree to which you are willing to take a step back and evaluate the various aspects of your own upbringing—the good, the bad, and, possibly, the ugly—is directly proportional to how honest and humble you are willing to be.

Have You Met the Groom?

When we practice discernment to identify what we as Catholics want for our kids, we will see more clearly why all of this self-examination matters. What does the phrase "raising your kids Catholic" mean to you? Does it mean you take them to church every Sunday? Do you send them through the hoops at your local parish to check all the boxes for the reception of the sacraments? Or is it about behavioral modifications, hoping your children make moral decisions? Is it ensuring that they stay on the straight and narrow and don't get into too much trouble? Or is raising kids Catholic about something deeper? We like to reframe this question: The question is not *where* you are guiding your children but to *whom*.

When we really think about it, we realize that raising Catholic kids is guiding young souls back to their heavenly Father and home. It's not about showing up for Mass each week or checking off all the catechetical boxes. It's not about controlling your kids' actions or lifestyle. It's not about a *what* but, rather, a *whom*. The Church is not the bridge between God and the faith; the Church is the bride.

Have you ever asked yourself how St. Peter, a hot headed and impulsive fisherman, became our first shepherd and pope with little-to-no theological study or background in leadership? Have you stopped to consider why God chose Saul (later, St. Paul), the one hunting down early Christians and dragging them to their doom, as our first great missionary evangelist? Why would he call this fisherman to build his church on or this murderer to become a martyr? Simply put, they knew that they were leading others not to a thing (the Church) but to a person (the Christ). It was their personal relationship with God that made offering their lives a joy-filled service and, eventually, a glory-filled death. They could lead the bride—the Church—*because they knew the Bridegroom*, Jesus.

How well do you know the Lord? How well do you *really know* him? Are you Catholic because your family was, or did it become a personal choice for you at some point, where you encountered the Lord (and his Church) and everything changed? Do you self-identify as a Catholic because that's all you've known or because it is a vital part of your life and being?

Rate yourself on how well you know Jesus—not the doctrines of the Catholic faith but its cornerstone, Christ himself. *That number is as far as you can lead your children into the depths and riches and tenets of the faith.* The good news is that you can always go deeper, score higher. We've met plenty of people (ourselves included) who love Jesus too little, but we have yet to meet anyone who loves the Lord too much.

Your children need to encounter and fall in love with the Bridegroom if they are going to relate to his bride, the Church. It may mean stepping out on your part—increasing your daily prayer, making a regular confession of your sins, going on a retreat, getting a spiritual director, dealing with the hurts and wounds of the past and your upbringing, having some hard conversations, and making difficult changes so that your life revolves around the Lord in a new way.

Are your kids worth it? We live in a time when culturally Catholic kids, teens, and young adults are exiting the Church in droves. The ones whose parents are committed to the Lord and not just the faith are firmly anchored to stay Catholic amid the storms.

We live in a time when culturally Catholic kids, teens, and young adults are exiting the Church in droves.

As parents, we must do everything we can to guide our children into a deeper relationship with Jesus. It takes work. It takes discipline. It takes safeguarding our own prayer life and setting a course for the future, but it also means dealing with our past.

As a Catholic parent and the primary catechist, you can teach your kids to pray, take them to Mass, model a sacramental life, serve, sacrifice, and do your best to temper your own humanity while unleashing God's divinity in your home and family. You can do everything in your power to point them to God and, ultimately, to heaven. In the end, you cannot control what they do or who they become; you can only model what you desire in them. It's the ultimate invitation to surrender, really.

This approach doesn't mean you'll have all the right answers, but it does necessitate that you pause and pray long enough to see if you're asking the right questions about your past and present as you chart your kids' futures.

Moving Forward (Practical Steps)

1. Identify any areas from your own upbringing that may need healing. Try a book like *Be Healed*, by Bob Schuchts (Ave Maria Press, 2014), to allow the Holy Spirit to bring awareness to areas you may need to take to a counselor or spiritual director.

2. Read and pray with the following verses:

   Train the young in the way they should go; even when old, they will not swerve from it. —Proverbs 22:6

   Have no anxiety at all, but in everything, by prayer and petition, with thanksgiving, make your requests known to God.

   Then the peace of God that surpasses all understanding will guard your hearts and minds in Christ Jesus. —Philippians 4:6–7

Tend the flock of God in your midst, not by constraint but willingly, as God would have it, not for shameful profit but eagerly.

Do not lord it over those assigned to you, but be examples to the flock. —1 Peter 5:2–3

Take to heart these words which I command you today.

Keep repeating them to your children. Recite them when you are at home and when you are away, when you lie down and when you get up. —Deuteronomy 6:6–7

3. Consider the role your extended family still plays in your life. If they have a strong presence, are they offering a voice that is consistent with your parenting philosophy and goals, or do you need to set stronger guidelines? Discuss as a couple with charity, not defensiveness.

4. Read what the Church says about the role of parents in the *Catechism of the Catholic Church*, especially *CCC* 2222–27.

5. If you didn't do it earlier, create a mission statement for your family that outlines what you stand for and what your goals are for your marriage, children, and home.

Closing Prayer

Holy Spirit, come and dwell within us. Holy Spirit, come and save us from ourselves. Lord Jesus, we give you permission to be our Divine Physician. Please, come and heal us. Lord, we need you. You are the way, the truth, and the life, Lord. Speak truth into the lies and wounds, the hurts and pains, of our past. Help us to forgive where we need to forgive, to heal where we need to be healed, and to rise up stronger and better for our own children. Grant us clarity in our discernment of the past, wisdom in the present, and hope for our future. By your grace, Lord Jesus, help us to shed any thoughts, approaches, or defaults in our parenting that are not of you and that will not lead the souls you have entrusted to us to heaven. We love you, Lord. Come, make us new.

3

Three Truly Is a Crowd

Marital Intimacy after Kids

It was a long February day. Overcast, cold (by Arizona standards), and, overall, unpleasant.

I (Mark) returned home from an exhausting trip and went straight into work for one of those days that we all enjoy from time to time. Unreasonable people, annoying emails, dropped balls, and disgruntled drama all reigned supreme on this particular Monday. To top it all off, it was Valentine's Day, and words like *joyful* and *romantic* did not in any way describe my state of mind.

It was a Valentine's recipe for disaster.

Love is supposed to be all about self-sacrifice and self-forgetfulness. Love is supposed to be about *the other*. In fact, we consistently tell our kids that if someone says, "I love you," but doesn't follow it up with self-sacrifice, *it ain't love*.

How ironic that in our Catholic tradition we celebrate the feast day of *St.* Valentine—a saint who was brutally clubbed and eventually beheaded—by giving flowers and chocolates and cards, which necessitate no true sacrifice of self or time. But I digress . . .

On this particularly gloomy Valentine's Day, Melanie had been at home with three stir-crazy kids all day, reading, playing, and doing crafts aimed at making (or salvaging) a Valentine's Day celebration for our marriage. She had worked for hours to ensure that the kids were taken care of and that we could celebrate our sacrament. By the time I arrived home, however, I was annoyed and just wanted to get away from people.

One of us wanted alone time. The other wanted quality time. We were not speaking the same (love) language at all.

I entered the house frustratedly anticipating that our kids would have destroyed it (as little ones have a tendency to do in a matter of minutes). No one was anywhere to be found—just noise and a mess. Markers were scattered all over the kids' table, and remnants of cut out paper lay beneath it on the floor as if a kindergarten art class had just let out. Cards were haphazardly strewn across the counter. Music and lights were on in the family room as well as in the back hallways.

I was so overwhelmed and stressed out from my trip and unending workday that I didn't understand the scene playing out before me.

"Who lit candles? Were the kids playing with the lighter? And who threw flowers all over the place?" I vented as I turned the corner to the master bedroom.

Had I, Bartimaeus the blind man, had eyes to see, I would have noticed that the "flowers" were actually rose petals, the music was very romantic, and the markers had been used by our kids to make Valentine's Day cards before they were dropped off at Grandma's for the night. I would have noticed that the lit candles made a trail to my teddy-clad wife, waiting to greet me with a glass of wine and a smile.

The Two Become One . . . Plus One, Plus One, Plus One, Etc.

So, how do we, as married couples, miss the signs along the way that turn the one back into two—two separate minds and lives and focuses?

When Jesus said that the two become one, he meant more than a sacramentally induced merge lane where a husband and wife share household responsibilities and chores. The Lord was speaking, too, about marital intimacy. The two don't just become one theoretically but physically as well. Marital sex becomes an expression—a singular expression—of sacramental love.

Sadly, however, for many couples, the arrival of kids signals the departure of intimacy . . . and we're not just talking about sex (though that's definitely a challenge, too). Those couples for whom sex was primary prior to kids make quick "connections" in desperation, and those who had little physical intimacy before tend to fall into even less, becoming ships in the night—passing by each other between feedings, diaper changes, and so on.

As one bad joke goes, marriage has three sexual seasons: triweekly to try weekly to try weakly.

The reality, however, is that a Catholic couple's sexual connection is intimately tied to both their prayer life and their sacramental life. To those following the Church's teachings on fertility and who are using NFP (Natural Family Planning), a vibrant sex life is both possible and plausible. Now, for those reading this book who believe NFP is just a modern term for the rhythm method, nothing could be further from the truth. We encourage you to check out the many good resources available on the biological and physiological realities of NFP.

(As a side note, we have used NFP joyfully and successfully throughout our marriage. We cannot speak highly enough about it. It allows the husband an understanding of his wife's cycle in a way that is genuinely insightful about how she is feeling as the days progress. Periodic abstinence has helped us learn alternative methods of communicating and being present to each other; in addition, it provides a sort of honeymoon period every single month of our marriage . . . something we look forward to, protect, and cultivate.)

The term *intimate* can mean different things to different people.

Perhaps the problem is in the phraseology. The term *intimate* can mean different things to different people. How does a married couple keep their love life passionate, their connection consistent, and the flirtatious fun present as more and more sleep-deprivation machines called kids enter into the mix?

Passion comes from the Latin word *pati*, which means "to suffer" (think: Good Friday). Now, consider how the world and secular culture define passion. How do stories and films demonstrate passion? It's fascinating to see the dichotomy between heaven's view and the world's view of words like *intimate* and *passionate*. Marriage is the visible expression of both terms, lived on a daily basis—whether or not the world (or your kid) is comfortable with it.

Healthy PDA: Parental Displays of Affection

"Eww. You two are *so* gross!" our ten-year-old daughter emoted in disgust. She had come into the kitchen and found us kissing. Well, deeply kissing. We'll be honest . . . it was hot.

Broad daylight. Eleven o'clock in the morning. Standing in the kitchen. May not sound sexy, but it was one of those really good moments. It was that "rom-com" kind of spontaneous kiss when your eyes meet and you are overwhelmed with gratitude for each other, you have ten seconds as parents to actually hear yourself think, and you just want your spouse.

It had been a fun morning. No work or stress or sibling arguments to settle. The kids were out of the room doing chores or playing. It was quiet. We were both well rested (how often can you say that as parents?) and had been sitting and connecting over coffee for an hour or so. Just two suburban parents in pajamas, hair in different zip codes and coffee breath ablazing. Not a particularly romantic setting or moment, but we were feeling very connected, and a little peck turned into a full make-out session beside the toaster when our daughter walked in and acted as though our kiss had perpetually blinded and scarred her. A Greek tragedy was playing out in our kitchen to Oedipal proportions. We didn't think it was that big a deal. At least she hadn't walked in on us during sex like her older sister had. That's a moment that will assuredly come out in counseling someday, but let's not digress.

We laughed and tried to validate but redirect our daughter, saying we understood why she thought it was gross but that, someday, if she's called to marriage, she would understand why it's important. She dug in her heels and stood her ground. Our little General Custer was not going down without a fight in that kitchen. She corrected us. She berated us. "You can't do that in this house. That's gross. You can't do that in front of your kids. You just can't. Just eww."

I (Mark) told Faith to go upstairs and get dressed and to bring her piggy bank down. Our little prude descended the stairs a few minutes later with piggy bank securely in hand.

"Get in the car," I said with a wry grin. I took Faith to her favorite retail store, which is an overpriced explosion of sequin-covered clothes, stuffed animals, and teens at the register trained to upsell kids stuff they don't need, yet parents feel too guilty to decline. I told my daughter to pick out a sleep mask. "It can be bedazzled, cheetah print, tiger striped, sassy as you want. I don't care which one. Just pick."

Faith was visibly confused but acquiesced to my request. After scouring the spinning racks, she emerged with a ridiculous sleep mask that simply read "Chill." I told her to bring the mask to the register, waited for the salesgirl to inform her of the ridiculous price, and then told her to open her piggy bank and pay for it with her own money. Though confused, she did as I asked, and we promptly left the store before we were talked into buying a furry llama throw blanket or a unicorn onesie. We jumped in the car, but before I had put it in reverse, she asked me the question I'd been waiting for.

"Why'd you make me buy an eye mask?" my little beauty quizzically offered.

"Well, sweetheart, you were so offended by your mother and me kissing and so outraged by what you saw, I wanted to offer you a solution. You see, someday you are moving out. It breaks my heart, but that's the reality. Mommy isn't. I loved her long before God gave you to us. She gets more beautiful every day, and I'm going to keep on kissing her . . . a *lot*. So, if that hurts your eyes and brain that much, just put on this beautiful new sleep mask and . . . 'chill,'" I offered with a sarcasm usually reserved for social media posts.

She rolled her eyes, but she got the point. She has never made another negative comment. In fact, she's since told us that she's thankful for "how we love each other." Apparently, she doesn't see that played out in other homes at parties or sleepovers. How genuinely sad.

Modern Intimacy

The word *intimacy* has been sadly hijacked in the modern era. It now conjures up images of lingerie stores or pharmaceutical solutions to certain romantic challenges. Honestly, one hears the word *intimacy* used more in radio and television commercials for erectile dysfunction than within a sacramental or emotional context, but that's a painfully myopic viewpoint.

In reality, the etymology of *intimacy* points toward something far deeper than intercourse. From the Latin *intimare*, *intimacy* literally means "to make the innermost known." Far more than a mere baring of bodies, intimacy reveals and bares the souls of a man and a woman. The physical expression flows forth from emotional and spiritual intimacy. Intimacy doesn't just offer a body or a physical "end." Marital intimacy is a gift of self, offering mind, body, and soul, and a new beginning that invites the Lord into an even deeper role within the relationship.

In this way, a couple's prayer is even more intimate than their sexual expression of love. For a man and woman to really, truly bare their soul with each other—asking for prayer, forgiveness, or mercy—takes the highest amount of mutual respect and trust. Trust is the result of knowing and believing that you are loved.

The amazing reality is that the better a married couple's prayer is, *the better and more amazing their sex life will become.* That's the gift God bestows when a couple allows and *invites* him into their lives and bedroom; everything is blessed beyond measure. The best sexual relationships begin with mutual trust, respect, and emotional intimacy. Sex really does start in the kitchen . . . through small acts of thoughtfulness and service (such as unloading the dishwasher, making a meal, taking out the trash, or cleaning the fridge). Those small acts of selflessness and kindness lead to physical intimacy.

You may be wondering, *Why all of this talk about inti-macy between husband and wife in a book about parenting?* That's a valid question. Intimacy—emotional, spiritual, and physical—is not only a crucial part of a healthy, holy mar-riage but also an invaluable part of your children's upbring-ing and formation.

Kids need to see their parents cuddle, make eye contact, pray together, kiss, flirt, and make time for their marriage. We live in a hypersexualized culture, where unhealthy forms of intimacy and sexual use are praised in movies, ads, and shows. If twenty-five years of youth ministry have taught us anything, it's that how much kids know about sex should not worry modern parents nearly as much as *where they are learning it from.*

Kids need to see their parents cuddle, make eye contact, pray together, kiss, flirt, and make time for their marriage.

Every cell phone is a portal. Every computer is an invi-tation. People can disagree as to what constitutes pornogra-phy, but a healthy, married example of passionate intimacy is the greatest antidote to what the world offers on screen and online. Ask yourself:

- Do you affirm your spouse in front of your kids for his or her talents, traits, gifts, and physical beauty?

- Do you show affection to your spouse in front of your kids—even if you're not the PDA type—because you know healthy affection is rare and needed and beautiful in today's world?

- Are you and your spouse playful with each other?

- Do your children see you still court, flirt, and date your spouse?

- Do you and your spouse build each other up with the words you use? Do the kids see you affirm and verbally praise the other?

- Does your marriage set the example of intimacy you want for your children if they are called to the Sacrament of Marriage?

Remember, we model for our children the kind of man or woman we want them to bring home. That's not just happenstance. If a girl is raised in a home where she sees her father dote on and serve her mother, she will keep the bar high for herself, trusting that "good men"—though rare—do exist. If a boy is raised in a home where he sees his mother respect not only her husband but also herself, he will similarly seek a woman of virtue.

Lessons from the Life Raft

Picture it: The waves are crashing against an inflatable raft adrift at sea. You, your spouse, and your (several) kids are huddled in the raft in fear as the waves swell. There are no rescue boats or helicopters in sight. Storm clouds are on the horizon. You hold out hope but are unsure of when a rescue might come. The kids are scared. Your spouse is visibly fatigued, trying to put on a brave face for the children. The waters might contain sharks, or they might not. You have no idea.

You pray. You pray harder. All you want is safety for your family.

Then, a massive swell overtakes and capsizes the raft. All of you are plunged into the water. Here's the question: *Who do you swim for?*

Survey the water. Let's say you have four kids, ranging in age from teenagers to an infant. Who do you swim for in this storm and in the possibly shark-infested waters?

This was the question that was posed to me (Mark) in spiritual direction years ago.

"I swim for the youngest, the one who can't survive for long on their own," I replied with a logical, commonsensical pride to the priest sitting across from me.

"Wrong," he responded in a pastoral yet enigmatic tone.

"What do you mean? Of course, I'd swim for the youngest and most vulnerable child," I retorted indignantly. I thought, *What does this celibate guy know about the love of a parent for a child?* In the conversation that followed, however, it became readily apparent that I was the one in need of a shift in perspective.

"Mark," he said in a strong, fatherly tone, "why wasn't your first inclination to swim for your wife?"

I was shocked and, frankly, a little irritated. Why would I swim for the other adult who is perfectly capable of treading water?

"Father, are you nuts? Of course I'm going to protect my children above all else."

"That's the problem, Mark . . . you still think these kids *belong to you*. You love and want to protect your kids and you should, but you and your wife are first and foremost. Your first inclination must always be for her and hers for you. These kids are God's before they are yours. He's got them in his hands. They are safe and they are good. Think of them as on loan to you both to raise up to know him, but they are his long before and ever after they are 'yours.'"

I'd never felt simultaneously more and yet less important in all my life. He was absolutely correct—a tad harsh, but correct.

The Sacrament of Matrimony elevates us—it elevates our love, our sacrifice, and our self-awareness. Once we get married, everything that is "right" in the relationship gets even better, but everything that is wrong or not dealt with is exposed and—if still not dealt with—made worse. Then, God sends us kids, and everything that is right in the relationship improves exponentially, but everything still wrong is brought to center stage and magnified.

So, what if we were truly intimate? What if we, as couples, daily and weekly in our conversation and prayer, made our innermost selves known to each other? How different would our families look? This is natural for some couples (perhaps those who have had positive experiences in their families of origin), but for others, sharing feelings with anyone—spouse included—is awkward and uncomfortable.

So, we're going to walk you through a few exercises that will help you practice emotional vulnerability and intimacy in your marriage. There is no right way or time to do these exercises. It's all about being humble and transparent—or *intimate*—with each other.

Taking Inventory

Individually, answer the following questions. Take 15–20 minutes to carefully consider and write out your answers; then come back together to see how your responses compare. Remember: this exercise is to give you a starting point with communication—not to cause conflict or trigger past hurts. Pray before and after you share your answers.

1. How does your spouse most like to spend his/her time, from your experience?
2. What is your spouse's greatest unfulfilled dream?
3. What is your spouse's overall life goal?
4. What is your spouse's greatest struggle?
5. What does your spouse pray about most fervently?
6. What does he/she dislike most about himself/herself?
7. What is your spouse's greatest fear (spoken or unspoken), in your opinion?
8. What topics do you avoid bringing up with your spouse, and why?
9. What's the first thing your spouse would change about himself/herself, if he/she could?
10. What is the most important thing in your spouse's life based on his/her schedule, energy, and actions?

11. How do you express your love to your spouse?

12. How does your spouse express love to you?

13. What is one thing you would be willing to change to ensure more quality time with your spouse?

14. Do you feel like you sacrifice for your spouse? If so, give three tangible examples of your sacrifices.

15. On a scale of 1 to 10, where would you rank the importance to your relationship of praying together?

Date Night

Go on a date. Get a sitter, if needed.

Rule 1: Choose an activity that affords time to talk (seeing a movie together might not be the best choice).

Rule 2: Don't talk about the kids.

Rule 3: Share at least one memory of when you were dating, one thing you love about your spouse, and one thing you want for your present and future together.

Moving Forward (Practical Steps)

1. Read and discuss 1 Corinthians 7:3–4:

> The husband should fulfill his duty toward his wife, and likewise the wife toward her husband. A wife does not have authority over her own body, but rather her husband, and similarly a husband does not have authority over his own body, but rather his wife.

Do you agree with and live by this statement, or is there any impediment keeping you from giving yourself fully to your spouse? Do you look at sexual intimacy as self-gift? Why or why not? Identify any inhibitors in trust, and communicate why they exist.

2. Read and pray Philippians 2:3–4 in light of the last question:

> Do nothing out of selfishness or out of vainglory; rather, humbly regard others as more important than yourselves, each looking out not for his own interests, but everyone for those of others.

3. Sit across from each other on the couch or in bed and pray 1 Thessalonians 5:23 aloud as a blessing over each other before you go to sleep or to start your day.

> May the God of peace himself make you perfectly holy and may you entirely, spirit, soul, and body, be preserved blameless for the coming of our Lord Jesus Christ.

Closing Prayer

Lord Jesus, lead us to greater intimacy. Help us to unearth a new passion in our sacrament and relationship. Help us to be more affirming, affectionate, and grateful for each other. Help us to honor each other in new and deeper ways—not only for what the other does but for who they are. May our time together be sacred yet fun, deep yet playful, simple yet profound. May every kiss, every held hand, and every embrace demonstrate our deep-seated sacramental love and eternal commitment to all we encounter. Mother Mary and St. Joseph, pray for us that we, like you, would be a holy

couple with a holy family and that our marriage would mirror the perfect love of the Holy Trinity to a world desperately in need of such a witness. Amen.

4

Dusting Off the Altar

Creating a Domestic Church

Babies are like drill sergeants, sent to push you to the very edge of physical and mental limits while simultaneously growing you in character and toughness. Small children are like little vampires who drain every last ounce of lifeblood from you. Preteens are like an accident happening on the freeway: you care deeply and pray fervently, but interaction is usually awkward and somewhat painful. Yet you continue to watch as the melee unfolds before your eyes. Teenage children are like hurricanes: they swoop in and clean you out, disappear, and then reappear only to swoop in and clean you out—monetarily and mentally—all over again. Young-adult children are like long-term financial investments; you hope you see a return on all you've put into them, with interest (grandkids).

Each season of raising kids is a glorious and unique challenge, isn't it? Properly viewed, children are not just gifts from God (which they unmistakably are) but also saint-making machines. Marriage and family will increase virtue in you in ways you would never seek for yourself. And that's the beauty of God's plan! Parenthood is how God blesses you *out* of your selfishness and floods your soul with love, all while reminding you how little you actually know. Parenthood is not a tutorial but a PhD-level crash course in humility.

Parenthood is not a tutorial but a PhD-level crash course in humility.

The challenge is, in those most trying times and seasons, to remember that opposition isn't always bad; it can stretch us beyond what we think we are capable of. Like a kite rising in the wind, opposition sometimes reveals our true purpose as parents.

A Sunday without Sprinkles: An Unholy Day of Obligation

It had been a long few nights. It was our close friends' wedding weekend, and we were both in the wedding party. We'd been celebrating for days. Last-minute gatherings, out-of-town visitors, the rehearsal dinner, ceremony, reception—you know the drill. Getting through all of that is challenging enough as a couple, but when you are also trying to dress kids up, do their hair, and deal with the consequences of having them up repeatedly past bedtime (with extended family feeding them sugar like pellets to lab rats) . . . well, it quickly descends into madness.

By the time Sunday morning rolled around, we were praying for the Lord to come . . . immediately. The kids were up early and stir-crazy. We dragged ourselves downstairs and collapsed onto the couch. Everyone needed something. Normal sibling annoyances were escalating. The milk had gone sour. There was "nothing to eat," though the fridge was full. It was barely 9 a.m., and the day was already spiraling. Neither of us was looking at Mass as a source of strength or grace but, instead, as a Vatican-mandated chore we would have to endure with amped-up little ones.

We both grew silent as we nursed our coffees and sought out our final functioning strand of patience. Melanie at one point actually uttered, "No one is allowed to ask Mommy for anything or say a word while she is decaffeinated." It was so raw (and so damned funny) that it was all we could do not to burst out laughing from sheer fatigue.

What was sad was that Mass—which is supposed to fill our spiritual tank as a source of God's grace (divine life)—was now looking like a painful chore. The opportunity was, at that moment, overwhelmed by the obligation, but we managed to drag ourselves and our kids to the evening service. It may have been Ordinary Time, but it sure felt like Lent. The hospitality was lacking. The music was average. The preaching was subpar. The lector was apparently illiterate (how's that for irony?). The kids were wiped, and we were annoyed.

But then we received Jesus and perspectives shifted. We started to understand the good that had come from us "fulfilling our obligation." We had demonstrated to our kids that this is important. We had made Mass a priority as a couple and family, and God blessed us for it. A peace came over us after Communion, and on the ride home, while the kids hit their physical and emotional limits, we just began laughing in the car. Everything would be all right. God was with us and within us. He knew we needed the Eucharist.

First Things First: Reordering Your Week

How to tie a shoe. How to ride a bike. How to make yourself breakfast. How to turn off the water to an overflowing toilet. How to change a tire. These are just a handful of life skills we have taught our children over the past couple of years. These skills, though important, are not necessarily "life and death." It's amazing how much time and energy we spend teaching things that will help our kids over the next fifty years but how little time we devote to things that have eternal consequences!

As a parent, you are no doubt aware of the unending list of tasks that fall under your ever-expanding umbrella of responsibilities. Modern-day parents not only are suburban chefs and chauffeurs, tutors and teachers, but are expected to have the answer to any imaginable question (that Alexa and Google can't answer, that is), all while surviving on little-to-no sleep—and that's just during the week! On the weekends, you get to wash laundry, shop for groceries, do yard work, attend sports tournaments, pay bills, and clean the house.

Then comes Sunday, "the day the LORD has made" (Ps 118:24), our day to rest, and, instead, we work crazily. Sunday becomes anything but restful for most Catholic parents.

Just getting to Mass—and through Mass—with the kids in tow, dressed appropriately, and unscathed by any meltdowns is a minor miracle. Of course, that won't prevent judgmental eyes glaring from the pews if you enter during the first reading or, God forbid, your child is wailing or has a tantrum. "Save your judgment there, Ethel. At least *we're having kids!* And at least *we're bringing them to church!* Now turn around before I break your other hip." And to think that's just Melanie's take. Just kidding.

Sunday becomes anything but restful for most Catholic parents.

It's worth thinking about the fact that God desires us as parents to make the Sabbath—weekly (Sunday) worship, prayer, and rest—the focal point of the week, rather than school and activities and housework. God, in his infinite wisdom, didn't want us to focus on Monday as the beginning of our work week but, rather, on Sunday as the beginning of our rest prior to work. He was and is inviting us to recalibrate our minds, hearts, marriages, families, and homes to make Sunday the axle that the rest of the weekly wheel spins around and is ordered toward. It's sad that in the busyness of kids and jobs and just plain-old life we can so easily forget the point of it all.

I (Mark) don't have the greatest memory. I'm constantly setting reminders on my phone and sending emails to myself so that I remember to do certain tasks, whether it's buying a few groceries on the way home from work or picking up a child from a playdate or a rehearsal. It's possible I'm just getting old, or perhaps the stresses of the day take my attention. Maybe I have too much on my plate and in my schedule. Regardless of the reason, I am a man in need of reminders if I'm going to get done what needs to get done.

I used to wonder if the Israelites had only short-term memory. I mean, every time I read the Old Testament, it seems as though God the Father is saying to them, "Remember *this* and remember *that*." They were told to remember the Sabbath (Ex 20:8), to remember the Exodus (Dt 5:15), to remember God's fidelity at the crossing of the Jordan and taking of Jericho (Jos 4:7), to remember what Amalek did (Dt 25:17), and so forth.

Long before Siri, God's children relied on his divinely inspired to-do lists. The proverbial string was constantly being tied around the Jews' fingers to help them remember. So why did God constantly warn them not to forget (Dt 4:9)? Why did the Father have to keep telling us to *remember*?

Put simply, God warns us to remember *because he knows we will forget*. We will forget to keep first things first, in our marriages, families, and homes. We will forget his faithfulness in times of suffering, his love in times of desolation, and his promise in times of drought. We will forget that he is always with us, that he fights the battle for us, and that he has given us everything we need to emerge victorious. When we "remember" God and his promises, his fidelity is no longer a distant memory but a present reality.

More Than Words

God knows that in the midst of our weeks and years—
whether they be joyful or sorrowful—we will need to be
reminded of his faithfulness. Consider our Savior's words
from the Last Supper in the upper room. Jesus' command
was, "Do this in memory of me" (Lk 22:19). The word
memory means more than "recollection." Jesus wasn't
saying, "Hey, guys, after I'm gone, why don't you all get
together and reminisce. Tell some funny stories, sing some
songs, check in with one another because accountability is
important, and then, you know, 'remember' me. Just think
about all the good times we had."

No, this new covenant would fulfill what the prophet Jer-
emiah had foretold hundreds of years prior (Jer 31:31–34).
In this new and everlasting covenant, we would "re-mem-
ber" Christ—become one (member) with him, again—
through the living bread of his living body (see John 6:35,
48, 51, 53–56). This was no misunderstanding, for even St.
Paul, not present in the upper room that night, confessed
over twenty years later that the tradition was handed on to
him orally (see 1 Corinthians 11:23–26).

Through the Eucharist, Christ remembers us and is literally with us, as he promised he would be (see Matthew
28:20). In doing so, he renews our relationship with the
Father, again and again. It's in this moment, after receiv-
ing the God of the universe in his most Blessed Sacrament,
more than at any other time in the course of our week, that
things are finally on earth *as they are in heaven.*

When we receive Christ's flesh in the Eucharist at Mass
every Sabbath (Sunday), we are fulfilling his directive to "do

this in memory" (see Luke 22:19). We are members of the Body of Christ, no longer figuratively or symbolically but physically and ethereally. *This* is how "heaven and earth are filled with his glory," as we proclaim with joy at every liturgy. *This* is how we worship God *on earth as it is in heaven*, by being in communion with him.

This is why the Father invites us to his table weekly, if not daily—that we might remember. Christ knows our suffering. The Cross is the eternal reminder that God understands our pain, but with that recollection the One who is timeless also offers us a timely solution in his Eucharist.

≳♡≲

"Do this in memory of me" is not just a command . . . it's an invitation.

༄

Even if you forget everything else in your weekly calendar or on your grocery list, even if age or stress or busyness leaves you wandering about aimlessly, remember this: The God of the universe invites you to consume his flesh and blood that you might be consumed by his love. He invites you to become a walking tabernacle. There is no higher affirmation in creation that the Creator could offer you or your children. The only question you have to answer is, "Will I accept this invitation to love and to serve?"

God would rather die than risk spending eternity without you.

Read the previous line again. Let it sink in.

"Do this in memory of me" is not just a command . . . it's an invitation. This invitation, which echoes and reverberates from the altar in your local parish every Sunday, must also echo and reverberate from within the walls of your domestic church, your home. Do you, as a couple, view your home as a smaller parish, where souls encounter God? Do your children view the home as a healthy and holy, safe and loving space? Is it a church, where they can be real and raw and still know unconditional love?

If so, keep doing what you are doing. If you're unsure, perhaps reimagine your home to become more of a domestic, suburban sanctuary of sorts.

Rethinking Your Home: The Three Altars

The Old Testament is fascinating when you read deeply into it. Constantly and consistently, you see people doing the same things: digging wells, building altars, and offering sacrifices. It's as though these were the go-to things before sports and Netflix. Anytime a major character such as Abraham, Isaac, or Jacob traveled somewhere and set up camp, they'd dig a well to cover their family's physical needs and build an altar to satisfy their family's and tribe's spiritual needs.

You see, for those who knew God intimately, sacrifice was everything. It simultaneously reaffirmed who God is and who we are not (false gods). Sacrifice on an altar both visually and psychologically kept everything in right order. It wasn't enough merely to *say* that God was first. No, they had to actually *do* something to demonstrate that their words mattered. Much like in marriage—it's easy to say, "I love you," but that love is shown through actions, humility, and sacrifice.

An altar was and still is a place of sacrifice. Imagine if your parish church didn't have an altar. It would just be a large, empty sanctuary, and focus would shift from the Lord to the preacher or the band. As Catholics, we hold true to our Judeo-Christian roots, featuring an altar of sacrifice at the front and center of every church.

To raise a holy family, our homes must become mini-churches. Every home actually has three altars, whether or not we realize it.

Altar 1: The Dinner Table

Do you view your dinner table as an altar table as well? As a sacred space where food and time, stories and lives, are shared?

God did. The table for the Last Supper was more than a dinner table; it was an altar of sacrifice. The altar in your parish church is the same. At Mass, during the second half we call the Liturgy of the Eucharist, you have a front-row seat not just for the meal but also for the sacrifice. Pull up a chair, Peter. Recline at the table, John.

We are called, as parents, to mirror what Christ did. We miss the most important daily moments of a stressful Monday or a mundane Thursday if we speed through life. But God is calling us to recapture those moments. God wants us not just to retake Sundays but also to dive into weekdays, too. Meals are the best way to do that as a family. Now before you point to sports or other extracurricular activities as reasons why this is impractical, ask yourself what is most important in your home. Perhaps it is time to reassess and reevaluate how you spend your days as a family while still beneath one roof.

When we eat together, we are fed as a family not only physically but spiritually and emotionally as well. Days are shared, wounds are healed, and life gets put into proper perspective again. Biblical meals, free of the modern conveniences of microwaves and DoorDash, took time. That prep and cooking time afforded souls an opportunity to connect. Sad your son doesn't want to talk to you? Involve him in the cooking. Disappointed your daughter is more into Instagram than you? Ask her to help you prep the meal.

When we eat together, we are fed as a family not only physically but spiritually and emotionally as well.

As the kids grow older, as activities and sports schedules become more challenging, get creative. Maybe have a late dinner together once or twice a week—something light after earlier snacks. Pick a night you can all go out to eat. On a day when there are no activities scheduled, plan to make a big meal. The point is, *make it happen*. Actions follow beliefs. If you say your family is most important, the weekly routine should reflect that, including the meal schedules.

Ask yourselves:

Do you arrange your schedules and activities to maximize family mealtime at least a few times a week?

Is eating as a family a priority, or has it become something that just gets fit in?

Do your kids look at mealtime as important or annoying, or somewhere in between?

For the dinner table to be an altar of sacrifice, all in the family need to join in to make that happen. Do your children participate in all facets of mealtime, from prep to cooking to setting the table to clearing and doing dishes? Why or why not?

Altar 2: The Coffee Table

Conversation has become a lost art form in the modern age. We seek the constant stimulation and validation that screens offer but cannot deliver. We don't open up our homes to friends and strangers as we used to. Coffee tables were once spaces we would gather around to join in fellowship and community, sharing stories and struggles. Now they're a place for our outstretched feet and remote controls.

How often are God's greatest gifts—your children—in the same room with you, yet everyone is watching a screen? Not that family movies and TV shows are bad; they can allow us wonderful time spent together. But how often do we sit and just talk anymore? How often do we break out the puzzle or family board game? Yes, board games have just as much potential to damage relationships as to build them up . . . but it's still worth a try!

If we could all get better at asking questions, our friends, neighbors, and family members would feel validated and affirmed. We would seek genuine, not virtual, relationships.

Ask yourselves:

- Do your Catholic friends and non-Catholic neighbors feel comfortable sharing space and candid conversation with you in your home? If so, your coffee table is a true altar of sacrifice. If not, why not? Dust off that coffee table and invite some people around it, weekly or monthly.

- Can we give a better example of connection to a screen-obsessed generation? What would it look like to actively seek more face-to-face interaction, eye contact, and validating conversation in your own home?

Altar 3: The Marriage Bed

We have already spoken to this in the previous chapter—take a look back if needed—but let's consider some questions.

Ask yourselves:

Has your master bed become a place where you zone out or dial in? Does your energy go to the television, a tablet, or a book on the nightstand rather than to each other?

Unwinding is necessary, sure, but if the bed has become just another couch of sorts, how are you giving yourself—your time, your attention, your energy and body—as a true sacrifice to your spouse?

Now, you might be thinking, *At that point of the evening I've got nothing left to give.* Okay, fair enough. What would it look like if you shifted your household schedule in order to get in bed thirty minutes earlier? What would it look like if you took the television out of the bedroom and eliminated all screens? A ten-dollar alarm clock would alleviate the need to have your smartphone at the bedside. Finally, what would it look like if the door locked at a certain time every night and the kids understood that "at X hour, Daddy and Mommy are off duty"? (As if parents ever go off duty, but you get the point.)

Consider these words from the letter to the Hebrews: "Let marriage be honored among all and the marriage bed be kept undefiled, for God will judge the immoral and adulterers" (13:4). Adultery comes in many forms. Emotional adultery can happen more easily than physical infidelity. Facebook can be a mistress. Netflix can be a cheating partner. If your heart and mind are more enraptured by a show or book than by your spouse, make it a priority to recapture what seems lost. Do whatever it takes to carve out intentional and intimate time. *Make your marriage bed an altar and your master bedroom a sanctuary.* Sacrifice yourselves for the other. Focus and refocus your attention on your spouse, and your kids will be forever blessed by your example.

Moving Forward (Practical Steps)

1. Pray Joshua 24:15. Memorize it and teach it to your children. Collectively, write it out and post it in your house in multiple places:

   As for me and my household, we will serve the LORD.

2. Survey your family calendar and schedule every month. Find a way to have dinner together at least three to four times a week.

3. Over the next few weeks, put a crucifix in every room of the house. Put a predominant crucifix above the

marriage bed to remind each other that the bed—like the Cross—is a place of self-gift and self-sacrifice.

4. Go online to www.vatican.va and look up St. John Paul II's apostolic exhortation *Familiaris Consortio*. Read it separately or together, and discuss it. Pay specific attention to sections 14, 26, and 39.

5. Make dinner as a family. Everyone participates in preparation and cleanup. During dinner, say a special prayer as a family, where everyone offers what they are thankful for in their lives.

Closing Prayer

God our Father, you have called us to greatness. You have called our marriage to stand out. You have set our family apart in the hope of drawing us and all we know closer to your perfect love. Make our home a sanctuary of peace and forgiveness, of laughter and love. Make our dinner table an altar of joy and mercy, our family room and coffee table an altar of understanding and compassion, and our bedroom and marriage bed an altar of purity and holy passion. Help us to model sacrifice for our children in the same way you modeled sacrifice for us in the upper room and upon the Cross. Pour out your sacred blood over our home, protect us from the evil one, and make our home holy as you are holy. Amen.

5

Striking a Chord

_____

Finding and Maintaining
a Rhythm of Prayer

We wait for it every year with eager anticipation. Fall turns to winter. Leaves descend. Temperatures drop. Trees and lights go up. Music changes. Lines lengthen. Anticipation grows.

As a couple, we wait not merely for Christmas but for the Christmas cards and photos and even the Christmas letter inserted by so many. It's become a modern Christmas tradition of sorts. Some families apparently long to give an update to loved ones and longtime friends about what their little rascals have been up to. Yet, inevitably, these letters serve to remind us year after year of how awesome others' kids are and (the subtext of) how everyone else's offspring fall short in comparison.

Now, to be sure, most of these Christmas letters are well intentioned and healthy. A sort of "Hey, we know we haven't connected much this year, so here's what our brood is up to" type of thing. There's nothing wrong with that tone and goal.

Then there are the other Christmas-card updates, which are 50 percent gloating, 30 percent embellishment, and 20 percent straight-up blind pride and narcissism, often veiled as humble joy and gratitude for having such perfect kids.

Those are the letters that make our eyes roll so far back in our heads, we ought to have an ophthalmologist on speed dial. C'mon, we all love our kids, but let's not pretend little Johnny is the next John Mayer because he managed to knock out "Hot Cross Buns" on the recorder. Let's regain some perspective, huh?

The Christmas family update might read something like this: *We were so blessed to see our little Connor flourish not only at every sport he played (and many he has yet to try) but also in music, arts, academics, and service. He was moved to second chair in band after his rousing performance of "When the Saints Go Marching In" at the school pep assembly. His art teacher said his painting of the Nativity was the most realistic she'd seen in thirty-four years of teaching. Connor's homeroom teacher said he might want to consider nuclear physics after he scored an 87 percent on his last math quiz, and when asked how he'd cure world hunger, he said, "Feed the hungry." Well, we just couldn't be more proud!*

You get the idea.

It's great to be proud of our kids. They are amazing, after all. They are assuredly gifts from God (see James 1:17), but have you noticed that underlying, almost passive-aggressive vibe that exists among some Catholic parents—in the stands at games or in pick-up lines, in coffee conversations or on Facebook—who tend to posture and compete over how wonderful their children are compared to others? It's usually subtle and often condescending, but always with a hint of self-deprecation and false humility so that no one can actually call them on it.

False humility is true pride, and our children should not see it modeled by their parents.

Parental Authenticity: A Lost Art Form?

For several years now, we have deeply considered writing our own little "Hart Family Christmas Update." While we've yet to get up the gumption to actually pen our snarky missive, it might (in theory) go something like this:

We were blessed beyond measure this past year. After Mark's last book—undeservedly in our opinion—became a New York Times best seller, we decided to celebrate in Calcutta, giving back to those who'd never been blessed enough to read it.

Soon after, our eldest, Hope, had a small picture of a horse she'd scribbled on a napkin at Chick-Fil-A auctioned off at Sotheby's for well into six figures, financing her collegiate aquamarine studies so that she can finally eradicate plastic straws and single-handedly save all of those precious sea turtles!

Our second oldest, Trinity, saved the life of a man who was having a heart attack in Hobby Lobby. After learning CPR from her time on TikTok, she successfully resuscitated him and kept him breathing until the paramedics arrived. Though only a freshman in high school, she's been offered a residency

at Johns Hopkins Medical Center and a spot as fill-in host on
The Dr. Oz Show.

Our third child, Faith, while still in middle school, recently
placed top ten in the country in her dance trio and is now
choreographing Taylor Swift's next Super Bowl appearance.
She was so thankful for the invite that she wept. Some of those
tears were stored in a vial and have been used to heal a blind
Tibetan and also a childless widow . . . who now, to date, has
eighteen children.

Last but certainly not least, our youngest, Josiah, just
turned seven. He's only a year removed from T-ball, but the
Yankees are scouting him for his ability to hit the slider, Nin-
tendo is considering him as a spokesperson for his proficiency
as a Mario gamer, and he is nearing a deal to play twins in
the Disney Channel reboot of The Suite Life of Zack & Cody.

As for us, we are just growing older and better-looking
. . . our waist sizes are the smallest they've been since we
were teenagers. We have the energy and stamina of World
Cup players; engage in deep, meaningful conversations (even
with kids in the room) nightly; enjoy a prayer life that takes
us to levels of ecstasy; and, after hours of sex, gently drift off
to sleep every night praying a Rosary in Latin because, you
know, why not?

Okay, this may be a slight exaggeration, but we do live in
a social-media-driven world. Everyone's life is a slight exaggeration by Instagram standards. So why does this matter?

Well, many parents we meet (if not most) feel as if they
are failing. Catholic parents often feel this the most deeply.
It's as though Catholic parents who are trying to get to Mass
and raise their children in the faith each day have an even

heavier burden. Whether the burden comes from others or is placed upon themselves matters little. The struggle is, indeed, real in this area.

We've sat with couples over dinner or drinks, and when the subject of faith and family or prayer comes up, the other couple naturally assumes that we must have it all figured out. They seem to think, *Mark works in full-time ministry, he speaks around the world and is on Catholic radio, yada yada. The Harts must have the best prayer life and holiest kids in the Catholic world!* Oh, how we wish that were true.

We have seasons when things are clicking on all cylinders and our family is in a great rhythm, sure, but most days it's a grind. We see other families at Mass or hear about things they are doing to unpack the faith with their own children and sit in awe wondering, *What are we doing wrong?*

There is no one form that works for every family.

The answer is likely nothing. Every family is different. Every family's challenges and crosses are different. That's why we aren't suggesting any one form of prayer to couples reading this book. There is no one form that works for every family. People can and should share what has worked for them, but part of the glorious genius of the Catholic faith is the many different forms of prayer beyond the sacraments. Don't care for the Rosary? Pray a Divine Mercy chaplet. Not a fan of silent meditation? Open sacred scripture. Journaling not your thing? Dust off the corporal works of mercy; get out and serve!

The key is to find what works for you individually, then as a couple, and then as a family. You'll no doubt need to adjust and grow with prayer (and different forms of prayer) as a family unit over time, and that's how it should be. As your family grows older, you'll see certain prayer forms stick and others fade away. Lean into what your family enjoys, but also continue to encourage forms of prayer they might not appreciate at first. The goal is to move toward a daily and weekly rhythm of prayer beyond just grace before meals and prayer at bedtime (though both are invaluable and should never be missed).

The prayer of the family, however, has to flow forth from the prayer of the couple.

Parenthood: Nonstop Work, Nonstop Prayer

Prayer, not sex, is what unifies a married couple. Prayer is what holds the family together—both prayer for and with one another. Prayer is the rhythm of life, actually. When Christians set up their day to revolve around prayer, great things happen. This is what St. Paul meant when he told the budding church in Thessalonica to "pray without ceasing" (1 Thes 5:17). It's not as though St. Paul expected everyone to be on their knees 24/7, ignoring children, their occupation, and normal human tasks. What he meant was to make everything a form of prayer.

When you are conscious of your blessings, God's presence, and his goodness, you can turn almost any daily activity into a prayer. Unloading the dishwasher, calling Grandma, making your bed, vacuuming the house, doing your best on your homework, using your imagination, and spending quality time as a family can all be forms of prayer if done with sacrificial intentionality and thoughtfulness. Do your kids see it that way? St. Paul would.

The prayer of the family, however, has to flow forth from the prayer of the couple.

I (Melanie) recall one particularly exhausting time when I tried desperately to see how I could recover my sanity and turn my harried actions into a prayer. I was at the end of a ten-hour day with three kids under six years old (with two in diapers). I was worn out. A stomach bug had worked its way through each of our girls, and I had hit my limit. Mark came home from work and saw that I was at the end of my rope. Trying to "fix" the situation, he went into joke mode, thinking that if he could make me laugh, everything would be okay. He was wrong.

"I've changed like forty-seven diapers today," I shared in an exasperated tone.

"Wow. That's insane! I'm so sorry, babe. Well, look at it this way . . . a few more and you'll have basically prayed an entire Rosary—one diaper per bead!" he responded quickly.

I appreciated the effort, but it was too soon . . . let's just say I didn't change another diaper the rest of the night.

Reflecting on it later, though, I realized there was truth to the statement, as flip as it seemed at the time (okay, it was funny later). I had begun feeling like a failure as a Catholic mom. My prayer life wasn't what it once was. I wasn't making it to weekday Mass . . . I was barely coherent for Sunday Mass! I wasn't praying my Rosary daily anymore. I rarely read my scripture devotional, and when I finally did stop to pray, I was so tired and out of it that I couldn't focus. I'd log on to Facebook and see all these seemingly perfect Catholic mommy blogs and family pictures. I'd read stories about epic prayer experiences where other families prayed the Rosary together all the time, and my kids were using a rosary as a climbing rope on the side of Barbie's Malibu Dreamhouse. What had happened?

When we first got married, we'd make it to weekday Mass at least a couple times a week together. We would pray during morning coffee and nightly before falling asleep. We talked about spiritual things and had deep conversations. We were so in rhythm with each other and our faith . . . and then kids came. Daily prayer rhythms became weekly, then monthly, and then sporadic. We had to adjust our spiritual expectations to a new normal. Daily Mass was no longer practical with tiny ones in tow; as the family grows, malleability is the key. Prayer begins to look different. Schedules, finances, housework, and stress all come into play and must be dealt with. Your spouse's needs may change. Kids' needs will assuredly change. Throw in long workdays, travel, and extended family drama, and before you know it, the one (couple) starts becoming two (people) again. For us, prayer became more reactive than proactive. The process was slow and subtle and deadly. We argued more. Our stress increased, not because of more mouths to feed but because we were not being fed spiritually. Step one was identifying the problem, but step two was the hard part: changing our daily rhythm (or lack thereof). We had to get back into rhythm, and fast!

When Chores Replace Prayer, Prayer Becomes a Chore

How important is prayer to your daily life, personally and as a couple? How important is it to your life together as a family? How far are you willing to go to ensure that your kids not only learn their prayers but learn how to pray? That they stop to intentionally pray in different situations and begin to revolve their weeks and lives around the Lord?

How hard are you willing to work? Let's say we offered you ten dollars to email us a one-page document about why you love your children. Few would take the time to do it as the time involved is hardly worth the money. But let's say we offered you five hundred dollars to do a write-up. Dozens—if not more—would sign up. Now, what if we offered ten thousand dollars, and people knew it was legit? Hundreds, if not thousands, would take us up on the offer, right?

The importance and urgency we place on something is directly proportional to the value we assign to it. The greater we value something, the harder we work for it. It's easy to say that something is important to us, but our (collective) actions will reveal that statement to be true or false.

So why don't we work harder on our prayer lives? Why don't we pray more as couples and as families?

- Do we feel like prayer doesn't really make a difference?

- Is it a lack of faith or trust in God the Father?

- Is it laziness or busyness or a refusal to slow down?

- Is it that we were never really taught how to pray growing up?

- Is it that we feel foolish asking or guiding others to pray?

It's probably a combination of these reasons and more. One problem we see often in couples is the unwillingness or inability of the husband to lead on the dance floor of prayer. Sometimes this is due to indifference. Sometimes it's due to selfishness. Sometimes, though, it's due to a man's awareness of his own sin and spiritual failings—his seeming ineptitude as the spiritual head of the household. Some Catholics, when they hear that the father is supposed to be the spiritual head of the household, become indignant, as though St. Paul's assertion (from Ephesians 5) is somehow sexist. Nothing could be further from the truth.

Being the spiritual head does not mean being holier. As holy as St. Joseph was, he was not sinless like the Blessed Virgin. No, to be the spiritual head means that the man sets a visible structure and tone that the faith is important, that Mass is not optional, and that prayer is essential for the couple and the family. Think about how different our culture and church parishes would look if married men took a more active, vocal role within their families and communities as spiritual role models and leaders.

"Practically" Praying

A few years back, our family gathered for our nightly prayer time before bed, and on this particular night it was our six-year-old's turn to lead. Once everyone was settled and the squirming had slowed down, she began.

"In the name of the Father, the Son, and the Holy Spirit. Amen." Then she paused for all of two seconds and proclaimed, "Jesus . . . you rock. Amen."

The other kids joyfully agreed, "Amen," and they all disappeared upstairs with the speed of a desperate jailbreak.

In the moments that followed, I (Mark) felt like a failure. I am a professional catechist, after all. Luckily, Melanie was there to help me refocus my perspective, as she does almost daily. As we laughed and processed what had just happened, something hit us: It's not about the length of our prayers; it's about the depth. Our daughter had actually demonstrated something sorely lacking in many adult prayers—a true relationship!

When you pray as a family, what are you modeling for your kids? Would they think of God as distant or near, untouchable or approachable?

In your personal and couple's prayer time, it's vital to remember that God doesn't grade us on length or diction. Words matter little if our intention is pure. Likewise, when leading prayer with your own children, it's important to remember that less is often more. Simplicity is a direct route to sanctity.

Do you remember that iconic scene in the comedy classic *Meet the Parents* when Robert De Niro puts Ben Stiller on the spot to lead grace at the family dinner table? Stiller offers a flowery verbal mess, beginning with evocative imagery of cascading fountains and ending with a quote from the Muzak version of "Day by Day" (from the musical *Godspell*).

Real-life versions of that scene sometimes play out when people attempt spontaneous prayer time with their family. I've seen it happen. Feeling awkward, we start to use big words or too many words. Like some English orator from the nineteenth century, we speak differently, slowly and dramatically enunciating multisyllable words and employing a complicated vocabulary to ask God for the simplest of things. It's like we are self-consciously on the witness stand where every word is being scrutinized. If your prayer tongue is poetic, and even flowery, that's beautiful. Praise God for that gift, but praise him with it at more opportune times than when trying to introduce your kids to an authentic and transparent relationship with the Lord. As the parent, you're not only leading prayer; you are modeling it.

When Prayer Vanishes, God Vanishes

So, why is it important to model prayer as a couple and to teach your kids to pray? Well, consider, instead, the natural effects of *not* having prayer in your life.

When you *don't* pray, you will . . .

Begin to doubt God's presence in your life.

Begin to doubt God's promises.

Begin to doubt God's faithfulness.

Begin to doubt God's goodness.

Begin to doubt God's love.

Begin to doubt God's very existence.

Some of you reading this right now may relate to some of these doubts. The good news is that these attitudes can change. Prayer is where the weight and burden of your cross changes shoulders. Stop for a moment. Open your heart. Ask God to be with you, right now. Breathe in God's peace. St. James told us, "Draw near to God, and he will draw near to you" (Ja 4:8).

꒒ꕥ꒔

If God feels distant, ask yourself who was the one to move away . . . him or you?

꒰ꔷ

The doubts we listed tend to emerge in the order given. Those steps make sense, do they not? When we aren't praying, we cease feeling as if God is truly present to us (although, in reality, it's we who are not being present to him). If God feels distant, ask yourself who was the one to move away . . . him or you? Scripture speaks of "the shadow of [God's] wings" (Ps 63:8) and "your shade at your right hand" (Ps 121:5). These images suggest not only solace and respite from danger or the scorching sun but also God's intimate proximity to his creation. Moments of loneliness and fears of abandonment are just the shade of God's outstretched hand; he is present to us even if we cannot see or "feel" him at that moment. As St. Catherine of Siena once said, "God is closer to us than water is to a fish." The problem is that we cannot see it that way if we aren't praying. When parents stop praying, their kids are in spiritual danger.

As we begin to doubt that God is truly watching and truly present, we start to wonder about the promises he has made to us. The Bible gives us more than four thousand of God's promises—that he will be with us, hear us, protect us, fight battles for us, and so on—but if God the Father isn't around, we can't take him at his word.

When we've come to believe that God is no longer a Father who keeps his promises, we start to doubt that he is faithful in big and small things. He becomes the absentee Father who isn't there for us and doesn't fulfill our basic needs. We feel rejected, in a way. The more estranged we, as parents, feel from God, the less we mention him in conversations to or around our children, and he becomes a distant (rather than intimate) being.

As God becomes more distant (in our minds), we project our feelings of hurt and negativity onto him. Not only do we doubt that he'll come through for us or fulfill his words but also we begin to question his character and heart. We doubt his goodness. If he is so good, why does he allow bad things to happen? It's the classic trap.

Once we go down that rabbit hole, we stop believing the core teaching of the gospels—namely, that God is love (1 Jn 4:8). Christ's entire life echoed this deepest, fundamental truth, but our hurt and sin blind and deafen us to this irrefutable fact. The longer we wait to go to Confession and receive God's mercy, the more the hurt deepens and the doubt grows. And when parents pull away, whether consciously or subconsciously, the entire family unit begins to pull away. Priorities shift, schedules fill, and, soon, rather than a household that revolves around—and finds its strength in—God, we become estranged from him.

Of course, if we refuse or fail to see God as love, we then begin to doubt his very existence. The slope has become far too slippery. There is nowhere and no way to stand. Atheism or agnosticism becomes the only logical alternative if the God we were raised (or more to the point, *weren't raised*) to know is not present or trustworthy or faithful or good or loving . . . well then, he just must not be real.

Maybe you've been through the stages of this thought process or are in the midst of it. Maybe your older kids are embroiled in the same dilemma. Prayerfully considering a series of pitfalls like this helps you to discern where you may be struggling with God. This shift in perspective will also help you diagnose your kids' depth (or lack thereof) on their journey of faith. It will also aid you in ascertaining where they may struggle with God's existence or trustworthiness as they mature.

So what are some practical things you can try (or keep trying) to build a more prayerful family culture?

Learning to Pray from the Ultimate Pray-er

When Jesus taught us to pray, he could have been far more ethereal in his speech, far more verbose, far more theologically high-minded . . . but he was not. Jesus was *simple* in his prayer; he was succinct. When Jesus gave us the Lord's Prayer (the Our Father), he communicated the depth and breadth of God's majesty and mystery in simple verses of adoration and petition. The same should be true of our approach.

Being more intentional about the simplicity with which we pray will not strip family prayer of its Spirit-led glory; it will enhance our prayer. It will empower our children who might be shy about praying aloud because they're afraid or self-conscious.

Teaching our kids to pray is not merely important—it must be primary. Prayer is more important than oxygen. Think about it: If you stop breathing, you'll see Jesus. If you stop praying, who knows who you'll see?

"Jesus . . . you rock. Amen."

Remember these simple parenting truths when teaching your kids to pray:

1. Embrace moments of silence.
2. Encourage them to pray aloud by modeling simple, direct language.

3. Introduce them to differing forms of prayer and various times to pray. Being consistent with daily prayer time is essential, but what the prayer looks like can change.

4. Exemplify what prayer is *and* what it is not.

5. Remember (and remind your family) that God cares about the depth of our prayers more than the length. It's

not about the words as much as it is about the posture of the heart uttering them.

Ask the Lord to simplify your heart, and your prayer will follow. It's great to pray, "Lord, I offer you praise and glory and thanksgiving, for you are the Lord, and there is no other." But don't be afraid to look up to heaven, smile, and pray, "Jesus . . . you rock. Amen."

Moving Forward (Practical Steps)

1. Ask each family member what he or she needs prayer for right now in their life. Everyone who is old enough takes a turn giving a response. Commit to praying for those intentions three times a day for a week, and then check back in with one another, allowing the kids to ask you how you are doing, too.

2. Fast for your spouse and kids once a day or once a week. Perhaps the fast is from coffee or sugar or snacking between meals. Commit to small acts of self-denial as a way to pray for your loved ones and to remain mindful of their needs.

3. Create a family prayer board and give it a prominent place in the house. On it write out specific intentions for your family, for friends (kids' friends, too), and for their families. Consider adding photos of those you are praying for, to make the board more engaging visually.

4. Read the Sunday scripture readings ahead of time. Find them in your parish bulletin or online on a Catholic app. Take time during the week to pray them with your spouse and, when your kids are old enough, as a family.

Spread the readings out over a few days, and on Sunday watch everyone engage more fully in the first half of the liturgy. (It may help, too, to listen to a podcast that unpacks the Sunday readings. You can find Mark's free podcast titled *Sunday, Sunday, Sunday* on iTunes and on biblegeek.com. You can also visit lifeteen.com and pick up a copy of *Ascend*, Mark's paperback book that gives an overview and background to the readings for each Sunday.)

5. Make a commitment to go to Confession as a family once a month. The rhythm of going together and praying while the others are making their confession is a tremendous gift and spiritual practice. It's unlikely teenage kids will come to you and say, "Mom and Dad, can you take me to Confession?" However, if going to the sacrament is a normal activity you do as a family, you give them the invaluable opportunity to receive God's mercy whenever they need it.

6. Try to pray a Rosary as a family. Perhaps you just start with one decade and build up from there. Maybe you and your spouse pray a Rosary over the course of the day when you are apart and then finish the final decade together in bed. The key is getting into a new rhythm, sticking with it, and building on it!

7. Take the time to look up these verses as a couple (or as a family) and highlight them in your Bible:

    1 John 5:14–15
    1 Chronicles 16:11
    Jeremiah 29:12

James 4:8, 5:13
Matthew 5:44
Romans 12:12
Matthew 7:11
Philippians 4:6
Colossians 4:2

Closing Prayer

Lord, grant me the desire to pray more.

Pray just that line, slowly, over and over and over again.

6

Screen-to-Soul Contact

———

Creating a Ministry of Presence with Your Kids

"You are ruining my li-i-i-fe!" she moaned into the couch cushion beside us. Crocodile tears streamed down her face, and her hair was matted against her fire-red cheeks. The anger, the frustration, the angst were almost palpable . . . it took all we had not to burst out laughing.

This performance made the actors in Hallmark Christmas movies look Oscar-worthy. Not to sound completely callous, but all of this—the melee and melodrama and prepubescent rage—was over our daughter's "need" for a cell phone and Instagram and Snapchat accounts. "I'll have no friends, no social life . . . and you don't even care," she wailed as though a countdown clock on her chance at happiness was ticking away. When we explained she was not going to get these things, you'd have thought we pulled out her beating heart and devoured it right before her eyes.

Did we desire to hurt her? Of course not. Our most ardent goal was to shield her from predators, from bullies, from "frenemies," from morons, from other kids whose parents didn't understand or care enough to protect them, and, ultimately, to protect her from herself and her need for the validation of others.

We had instituted strict rules in the Hart house. No personal screens, only a shared computer or iPad in a public space (with filters and no private password), and no cell phone until graduating eighth grade and preparing for high school. No social media until well into high school, and even then, any account would be set on private mode and reviewable by us daily. Retaining an account would depend on our kids' ongoing grades, overall attitude, and emotional maturity.

Undoubtedly there are many parents reading this book who disagree with these parameters, but this is what we prayerfully decided would work for our family, and we have seen it bear tremendous fruit in our home.

To be clear, every modern parent is waging a war for their children's souls whether or not they readily see or admit it. One of the single greatest battles in this war is the battle over screens. It's an ongoing conflict with no end in sight. It was a battle we were expecting but were not fully prepared for when we found ourselves embroiled in it. No, this battle would not be solved in a matter of mere days or weeks; it would span years ... *per kid.*

Those with preteen and teenage kids know it well. Those with younger children or those awaiting kids ... brace for it. The Old Testament speaks frequently about false gods made of gold and silver. The only twenty-first-century difference is that our false gods have screens and pixels. Our children have always known a world with the internet. They are the most connected and yet disconnected generation in history. They can access unfathomable amounts of information with lightning speed yet lack focus. They are perpetually communicating with others virtually yet feel isolated. They are more affirmed than any generation before them, yet they constantly seek validation.

─ॐ─

The only twenty-first-century difference is that our false gods have screens and pixels.

∽

They are surrounded by conflict, both genuine and contrived (again, online), but many lack the skills to resolve tensions with their peers. They become overwhelmed by the false courage that hides behind posts and screens and become mired in passive aggression, sarcasm, and the "sorry, not sorry" culture of verbal abuse. How do we parent a screen-based, screen-obsessed generation successfully? How do we help our kids discern and sort out the actual drama that deserves their attention, prayer, and response and guide them to avoid the emotional minefield that is just adolescent angst played out in their circle of friends? How do we win the increasingly growing battle of the screen?

Let's begin by considering a few questions.

Does your child have access to a phone or other screen for multiple hours a day?

Are there clear and set rules in place in your home as to the total amount of time each child is allowed to be on a screen each day?

Do you have appropriate monitoring software or other measures in place to analyze, limit, and, if necessary, physically prohibit screen time and exposure?

Do you have constant access to your children's password for every device?

Have you established a specific time when said devices are placed in a separate location (outside of their bedrooms) at night?

Have you clearly communicated to your children that you will review their texts and social media accounts at will to see what is filling their streams? Do you have access to do so?

Do your children have any alternate accounts on Instagram, Snapchat, etc., where they can post images and messaging? Would you even know how to check?

These questions are not meant to cast suspicion on your kids' behavior or their sense of responsibility in using screens. The purpose is to help you see if there are any gaps in your perspective or blind spots that may be worth taking a look at. Many of the fights that occur over screens result from our failure to set clear lines and expectations. Even if your child has had their device for a long time, it's not too late to do some retroactive parenting and set new parameters, such as "no phones at the dinner table or in restaurants," "phones in the kitchen at night, not in your room," "all passwords are known by Mom and Dad," and so on.

The screen battle is often lost because we, as parents, cannot keep up. Technology changes far faster than we can keep pace with. It's often easier to take the path of least resistance. In our desire to pacify our children or make them happy, we hand them a tablet or a phone too soon, and while they can operate certain devices and platforms far better than we can, they are not emotionally or spiritually mature enough to properly navigate all of the situations they will find themselves in. Remember that when we hand our child a smartphone, we are actually handing them a personal computer that also happens to make calls. Without proper safeguards and filters, we have handed them access to the seven deadly sins emanating forth from the screen's white light.

So how did we get here as a society, and how in the world do we pull ourselves out of it?

How Quickly Things Change

I (Mark) remember when we used to teach people not to get into cars with strangers, and now we frequent Uber and Lyft. Kale used to be merely a garnish placed around other food, and now it's a superfood eaten with joy. People used to burn CDs or illegally download music, and now everyone uses Spotify or Apple Music. If you wanted to watch a movie, you headed to a video store; now you tune in to Netflix. If you wanted to be famous, you needed more than a YouTube channel. When I was growing up, we had only four television networks (and channels), people got their news from the paper, every home had an answering machine, few people recycled, and smoking was still allowed indoors. Even courtship has changed. We used to have to walk across a room, make eye contact, and start a conversation that would hopefully result in a name and a phone number . . . now people just swipe left.

Although I know I sound like that grumpy old man down the block yelling for those "darn kids to get off our lawn," I am actually a fan of tech, apps, and social media. Melanie, however, is not . . . not at all. Getting to a point where the two of us agreed on screens and media usage took a lot of conversation and back-and-forth communication. I love the freedom and ease that the internet, smartphones, and various tech platforms can bring to tasks. I hated going to Blockbuster to pick up a movie. I couldn't stand being stuck in a room where people were smoking, and I still think kale is gross, but I digress.

I (Melanie) have a very different take on technology usage than Mark. I have seen many friends' families and extended families scarred and have been surprised at how quickly marriages and homes can fall apart through the misuse of technology, social media, and the world of virtual reality. Emotional abuse and infidelity, bullying, body-image issues, heightened stress, suicidal thoughts, and depression are just a few of the byproducts of rampant and unmonitored screen use. I often feel as if people don't know how to talk to each other anymore. Everyone becomes more self-absorbed—obsessed with being seen and affirmed and validated by others—through a screen, rather than being present to someone sitting across from them in the same room. It's not just pornography destroying marriage and families but screens in general.

So, as a couple, we've had to consider our distinct perspectives on technology and discuss both the opportunities it creates and the dangers it presents. We've also had to balance the desires of our children, while recognizing what's at the root of those desires.

Kids want attention more than anything else, and while the attention they receive via screens may be what they emotionally crave, it is not the kind they genuinely *need*. Phones and social media offer our kids the immediate and constant validation that everyone seeks (adults included, even if we don't admit it). It's easy to get frustrated with our teens and preteens about their constant desire to be on their device, but when we look at where the desire is actually coming from, we can have more patience with our kids and ourselves. They just want security and affirmation, and it's our job as parents to figure out how to "fill their cups" so that they don't turn to social media for that satisfaction. That's just one question we've had to consider as parents.

But it's also about how we communicate with each other in the family. Virtually every parent we know wages the battle of the screen on an almost daily basis. Perhaps you, like us, have even gotten to a place where you've texted a child who is in another room because you didn't want to yell upstairs or go track them down! For all the potential good that comes with devices—such as access to research for homework and the ability to connect with friends and family members far away—there comes just as much or more potential for bad, such as online bullying, pornography, a general demise in normal communication skills, and a growing social ineptitude. Most young men, for instance, no longer have to make eye contact with a young woman, ask her name, or nervously flirt, much less summon his courage and invite her out verbally on a date. The timeless coming-of-age moments of courtship are now relegated to a text message or Snapchat for a majority of young souls. Actual face-to-face conversation has, sadly, become a lost art form for too many adolescents.

So, how do we—as parents—guide our teen and preteen children through the minefield of social media, the bombardment of screens, and the constant barrage of overstimulation? We have to begin not with a screen but with a mirror.

Out of the Minds of Babes

A few years back, a group of grade-school children were assigned a fascinating project: They were told to come up with an idea for a new app. The app could be anything they wanted, but they had to work together to agree on one idea. After a lengthy discussion, the kids decided on one concept they all felt strongly about.

The app they wanted to create was tentatively called the "STEL app", which stood for "Stop Texting, Enjoy Life." What did the app do, you ask? Well, it wasn't for the kids' phones or tablets—it was an app to be downloaded and installed on their *parents'* phones. It was a voice-recognition app that would immediately put the phone to sleep or in standby mode when it recognized the child's voice saying their mom's or dad's name. Isn't that sadly fascinating? When given the chance to create an app that could do anything, these young souls desired nothing more than the full and undivided attention of their parents at home.

You might be thinking, *Well, my kid is obviously not in that class; she's glued to her screen,* but whether your child is glued to their screen has precious little to do with whether you are glued to yours. Or does it?

I (Mark) have spent twenty-five years working in youth ministry. When people ask me what are the hardest conversations I have with teens, they are rarely about sex or pornography or same-sex attraction or gender dysphoria. (Those are delicate talks, to be sure, as I sit with a teen and try to unpack the Church's wisdom on the subject with patience and mercy and charity.) No, the most gut-wrenching conversations I have are with teens who come from good homes and good families, who often have both parents still under their roof, but who tell me that their parents are not present to them emotionally.

I was physically present, so by extension I thought I was emotionally present.

I've certainly made this mistake over the years. When I began traveling across time zones for work, I came home beyond exhausted. I thought I was being a good dad because I was home. I was physically present, so by extension I thought I was emotionally present. Yet I was constantly checking my phone or feeling the need to respond to a text or an email. The look in my kids' eyes showed that they had started to believe the modern lie—that the person on the other end of the phone or other side of social media was more important to me than they were. I needed to reprioritize how I set up my day and my life.

It's sadly ironic that the more wireless we get, the more difficult it becomes to actually unplug. There's always one more email to check or one more text to rattle off. Face-to-face conversations have been replaced not with calls but with texts and, increasingly, not even texts but emojis. It's easy to get sucked into that work vortex where—before you know it—you've been in a room with someone, twenty minutes have passed, and not a word has been spoken. And it's tempting after a long day to just log on to Facebook rather than strike up a conversation with a child you fear may have no desire to talk to you.

But they do want to talk to you. Your children are dying to talk with you.

So, what is the secret? Why is it that so many kids act as if they don't want to talk to their parents, and what can we do to change it? The way we interact (or don't interact) with our children may be part of the problem. Let's ask a few hard questions.

"At" Is Not "With"

1. *Ask yourself: Do you talk with your kids or at your kids?* Are you asking them open-ended (rather than yes/no) questions, or are you speaking "at" them about things they need to do or not do?

2. *Do you model presence to your kids when you're together in the car, at home, or out running errands?* Do you silence your phone and put it out of sight when you're

interacting with your kids? Do you ask questions about their days and lives? That is the Gospel. Jesus came and dwelt among us. He laughed with us; he made eye contact with us. When we show interest and care to our spouse and kids, or even to the stranger standing before us, our attention is incarnational; we are being Christ to them. If your child's presence is important to you, then model it to them.

When we show interest and care to our spouse and kids, or even to the stranger standing before us, our attention is incarnational.

3. *Do you ever "waste time" with your teens?* Do you ever just plop down next to your kids on the couch when they're watching something or take a seat next to them at the counter and talk—with no agenda, no list? Does it happen daily? Self-gift is not a one-time thing; it's a constant challenge and invitation. As Christians, we are called to give of ourselves, taking everyday opportunities to attend to one another's physical and spiritual needs. That's what Jesus did; he ate with sinners (and he still does . . . at every single Mass). The better we get at talking about normal, inconsequential, everyday things with our kids, the more open they will be when we have to talk discipline or depth or faith.

4. *Do you know what your children want and need prayers for every day?* This last question might seem like an odd departure from the previous few, but if we don't know the answer, are we *really* present to the souls God has entrusted to us?

Not only do we have to learn how to be present to the loved one in front of us but we also must learn to be attentive to God throughout the course of our day. This is an ongoing challenge. You might be killing time between meetings, boarding a flight, or sitting in a coffee shop, but rather than turning to God for a moment of prayer or even looking up to see what's happening around you, you go into default mode and turn to the phone or computer. Have you ever stopped to consider that the quiet you so desperately crave as a parent may be available in those small, random moments you choose to fill with a screen?

Whenever you have a few moments to yourself, whether driving alone in the car or waiting in line to pick up your kids, pray and ask God for his perspective about your life, marriage, and family. Often in these seemingly ordinary moments, God speaks clearly and loudly. When we make ourselves present to him, he can be present to us and reveal what we desperately need to hear. It's as if the moment your screen goes dead, your soul comes to life.

Ever Present

Little did the apostles know prior to that Holy Thursday night the gift that God the Father had in store for them at the Last Supper. There was no way they could have fathomed—even with knowledge of the Old Testament prophecies—what a profound and inestimable thing was about to take place when Christ instituted his priesthood and gave them the Eucharist as his enduring and true presence.

It's as if the moment your screen goes dead, your soul comes to life.

Here was Jesus—Emmanuel, meaning "God with us"—offering not only his flesh and blood but his eternal presence. This is how he would fulfill his final promise in St. Matthew's gospel to "be with us always." This is how he would not only feed us as God's children but also model for us what it means to be parents—fully present all of the time. The Eucharist is more than a profound gift; it is a lasting invitation and challenge to all of us to do and become the same: fully present. If you stop and think about it, the Eucharist—Christ's true presence, body, blood, soul, and divinity—is the highest affirmation God can give his children this side of heaven. The Father is saying he wishes to dwell, not merely beside us, but *within us.* There is no higher affirmation possible than God humbling himself and taking on the appearance of mere bread and wine that he may dwell within us as we seek to dwell in him. By extension, adoration of the Blessed Sacrament offers more insight into the Father's heart—the opportunity to be mentally, emotionally, and spiritually present to God as he is completely present to us.

Carry that image a step further now, to your own parenthood. Consider the last few occasions you spent time with your child one-on-one. What did you talk about? Schoolwork or screen time? Chores or grades? What was the last compliment you gave them? What was the last action (other than an assigned task) for which you affirmed them? Perhaps this last question is easy to answer because you affirm them frequently. If it's taking you some time to respond, though, that might be the Holy Spirit convicting you.

True affirmation of our children must extend beyond praise for an accomplishment or honor. We don't want our children to feel as though their affirmations are performance based. If we limit our praise solely to when our kids do something well (a good grade, an achievement in sports, etc.), they begin to judge their value in our eyes according to their performance, and they could soon adopt that view of their heavenly parent as well. When we model the Father's love for us—unearned, unconditional, freely given—we teach our children that their worth is inherent in who they are and not what they do. It's good to demonstrate our love through affirming speech or small notes (even an unexpected text of love—for the older kids), and we should, but what is even more vital is our consistent presence and availability to our children . . . *that is true affirmation.*

Things have changed, to be sure, over the past few decades, but God's desire for us as his children and from us as parents has not. Kids seek companionship, affirmation, validation, and attention from those they love most. If they don't get those things from their parents, they'll look elsewhere, in friendships and online. God wants you to be that voice and guide for your children; that's why he entrusted them to you.

So, power down the phone. Plop down on the couch with your kids. Thanks to technology, you can enjoy watching a movie with them on any platform without driving first to the video store. Better yet, take a walk or a ride with your children away from all the screens. Remind them how much you love them and how thankful you are to be the one God chose to raise them.

Never forget that true affirmation, true love, is spelled "t-i-m-e." The gift of presence is the greatest gift any of us can give our kids. It's a gift that resounds long after the Lord calls us home. In a way, our presence to our loved ones now ensures that our spiritual presence will endure for decades and generations to come. Your time is more valuable than any smartphone . . . so give them the most valuable thing you have: yourself. That's what Jesus did.

Moving Forward (Practical Steps)

1. Pray with the following verses. Discuss what they mean to you as parents and as Catholics.

> The LORD is our God, the LORD alone! Therefore you shall love the LORD, your God, with your whole heart, and with your whole being, and with your whole strength. Take to heart these words which I command you today. Keep repeating them to your children. Recite them when you are at home and when you are away, when you lie down and when you get up. —Deuteronomy 6:4–7

And behold, I am with you always, until the end of the age.
—Matthew 28:20

2. Over the next week, as soon as you come home from work or all the kids are home from their activities, make it a point to put your phone away in a drawer for the night and model fully conscious presence to your entire family.

3. Challenge your children to make eye contact whenever they speak to you. If they are not looking when they ask you something, playfully refuse to respond until they do.

4. Take your entire family to adoration of the Blessed Sacrament at your parish and sit silently in the presence of the Lord. Begin small, with maybe fifteen or twenty minutes (depending on the ages of your children), and build from there. If your parish doesn't have an adoration chapel, find one within driving distance. Consider asking your pastor to schedule time in your parish, perhaps monthly, for this ancient and beautiful form of prayer.

5. Have a family affirmation session. Take turns passing something symbolic (such as a battery-powered candle) from one family member to the next. Everyone takes a turn offering a sincere affirmation to the person holding the object. Offering these affirmations not only validates your loved ones in a healthier way than any "like" or comment through social media but also demonstrates an appreciation for Christ within them.

Closing Prayer

Lord, you are ever present to us even when we are too self-absorbed or preoccupied to notice it. Help us, dear Jesus, to see your face in the faces of those around us and before us, each day. Help us to be present to the moments of life that pass by so quickly, never to return. Help us as parents to hear and acknowledge, to witness and validate, all of the joys and pains our children experience daily. Grant us awareness to see them, wisdom to guide them, and strength to accompany them through the trials of life. Send mentors, peers, and friends to help us guide these beautiful young souls along their journey back to you. May the Holy Family pray with us and for us until you call all of us home. Amen.

7

Holier Than Thou

Raising Future Saints

Have you ever thought about how St. Joseph must have felt each day? Think about it. Guys, put yourself in his sandals for a minute. You're raising God and married to a woman who literally never sinned. Talk about "Mrs. Right."

Had the great St. Joseph not been a picture of humility, you'd better believe he would have been the most annoying father in Little League history, constantly telling the coach, "Put my kid in . . . he's God!"

Imagine Jesus shooting an eighteen in golf, never striking out in baseball, and running across the pool at the swim meet. Imagine St. Joseph trying to teach Jesus how to fish—throwing his net to the wrong side of the boat and having a young Messiah quietly shaking his head and saying, "No, Dad . . . off the starboard side."

Imagine modern-era St. Joseph at Jesus' first high-school football game, sitting next to the Blessed Virgin in the stands, wearing a #1 or #3 jersey (what other number would Jesus wear?), cheering on their boy to victory as he tosses a touchdown pass . . . to himself on a play we call the "Hail Mary" but that he knew merely as "Rejoice, Mom!"?

It's ridiculous and impossible to imagine because the Holy Family seems so perfect, right? Whenever we hear our parish priest talk about Mary and Joseph as our role models, sure, we know he is right theologically, but how exactly is that supposed to play out *practically*?

I (Melanie) know we want to be a holy family, but let's be honest . . . I'm not immaculate. Most days, I'm lucky to make time for a shower. Hair thrown into a messy bun, no makeup on my face, sporting yoga pants, I'm not a "picture of perfection" but, rather, a "polaroid of preposterous"— running late to pick up the kids from school or transport them to activities. I work nonstop all day and still can't figure out what I've even accomplished! I'm part chauffeur, part medic, part tutor, short-order cook, full-time counselor, and full-time cleaning lady who is expected to be a model of patience and virtue and have enough neurons left at the end of the day to be present to my spouse. Holy crap, that's hard. I used to think, *How can the Blessed Virgin really understand my life?*

I'm not a "picture of perfection" but, rather, a "polaroid of preposterous."

I (Mark) relate the same way to St. Joseph. I mean, I feel connected to him because he was married to someone *way* holier than he, but, come on, he was still the holiest dude on the planet. If not, why would God entrust him to emulate and model true manhood to his only Son? Did you ever think about that? Out of all the guys on earth, God looked down and said, "That's my guy! Joseph of Nazareth." His humility must have been otherworldly. How in the hell could I—or any man—meet that standard?

So, the question becomes, How do we—who are not (yet) saints—raise saints? How do we remain steadfast and hopeful and intentional about how we raise our kids in virtue? How do we stay positive even on the nights and days that quickly get swept away into the negative? How do we not only survive the tantrums but thrive amid the hormone changes, the drama and melodrama, and everything that comes along the way? How do we not lose our joy in the struggles of the day and the seasons of life we cannot control?

The answer is all about allowing God to widen and change our perspective. You've probably noticed by now that we have mentioned perspective throughout this book; that's because it's often what separates true parents from mere caregivers and babysitters. *Perspective* is a fascinating word, etymologically speaking. It comes from two words in Latin: *per* (meaning "through") and *specere* (meaning "to look"). So, quite literally, having the proper *perspective* is not so much looking *at* a situation as it is looking *through* a situation. God desires to help his children capture or regain perspective if their hearts are humble and trusting enough to let him do so.

The Israelites saw the Red Sea, but God and (soon) Moses saw a path through it. Saul's army saw only the unconquerable Philistine warrior, Goliath, but God and (soon) David saw the Philistine's arrogance and blasphemy. Simeon foretold great suffering accompanying the Messiah, but God and Mary knew well that suffering would be the path to salvation. The question is whether you trust God when you can't see the broader picture. The question is whether you can look "through" a situation or period of hardship as a sinner pursuing sainthood and help the young souls entrusted to you to do the same. It's about adopting a wider view, stepping out of the moment and recognizing the various seasons of parenting, and distinguishing the short-term traumas from the long-term goal.

D-Vine Intervention

It's our absolute favorite time of the year. No, not Christmas, but our annual visit to the holy land . . . of Napa and Sonoma. Okay, so maybe it's not the one, true holy land, but, for us, a few days away from work and kids and screens and distractions, just strolling through vineyards, sleeping in, eating well, sipping fine wine . . . it's a small taste of heaven. Much like Adam and Eve before us (though with more clothes), God meets us in the garden or, in this case, the vineyard.

One fall day, during harvest, we were visiting a lovely winery. The afternoon prepared to turn to evening. We had enjoyed an oh-so-excruciating day of wine tasting, taking selfies, and avoiding calls from the grandparents who were taking care of our beautiful yet quarreling angels back at home. We sat on a gorgeous patio watching the sun as it set on the western mountains, and we imbibed an incredible pinot. Tired workers who'd been picking grapes under the hot sun began, one by one, to empty their bags and clock out for the day. Their hard work was inspiring. It almost made it difficult to sit and lazily enjoy wine . . . almost.

After a while we noticed that all the workers had departed except one. Even as the final rays of sunlight flickered across the valley, the last worker continued to pluck grapes off the vine. He never seemed to tire. The nameless, faceless worker was on a personal mission, it seemed. Whether attempting to win an employee-of-the-month award or some other honor, he kept going until there was no light left to work under.

Then we saw something that amazed us. Rather than exiting the way his coworkers had, this upstart emptied his bag and walked up the steps toward the patio and tasting room. He disappeared into the back only to reappear quickly with a fresh shirt, clean hands, and a smile. He began pouring wine for those still tasting and savoring the minutes before closing time. Forget employee of the month; this dude was gunning for employee of the decade.

I (Melanie) was struck by his patience with everyone— even ridiculous customers—after such a long day. As a mom, I could certainly learn a thing or two from this man's diligence. Meanwhile, I watched Mark, as boss and leader, marvel at the man's work ethic. We were both wondering what this man knew that we didn't.

To say we were captivated would be an understatement. We asked one of the servers if there was a manager or owner we could talk to just to praise this wonder worker in our midst. The server laughed and enlightened us. The vineyard worker/wine pourer in question *was the owner*! Dumb-founded, we invited him over to our table.

I (Mark) asked him, "How do you do it? How do you work the field like that with such tenacity and then come up here and deal with customers and manage staff? I mean how do you balance all that with such a smile on your face? That's a lot of work."

He looked at us almost quizzically and replied, "Oh, this isn't work. I'm the luckiest guy on earth. I love what I get to do. You see, I'm not picking grapes . . . *I'm making wine.*"

It was a moment we go back to often. Simple, yet profound wisdom shared not as a proclamation but, rather, as an invitation.

As parents, it's easy to lose perspective, isn't it?

As parents, it's easy to lose perspective, isn't it? Parenthood has a funny way of reprioritizing your life in ways you would never attempt on your own. Your life is no longer yours. Stresses mount, be they financial or work related or family related. The kids' sleep schedule, school schedule, and activities schedule all become your schedule now, too. It's easy in the midst of the stressful Monday, mundane Wednesday, or overscheduled Saturday to lose sight of the long game of parenting and see only the work. We get so tired from the long and laborious days of picking grapes that *we forget we are making wine.*

Have you gotten to that place in your parenthood where it's tough to maintain perspective? Ecclesiastes reminds us that "there is a season for everything under the sun." In fact, throughout scripture, we see the seasons dictating the people's daily way of life, from farming to trade to the waging of war. Seasons contain a natural ebb and flow, with birth and death, joy and pain, hardship and blessing. Still today, our Catholic liturgical year is broken into seasons. Whether Advent or Lent, Christmas or Easter or Ordinary Time, it's as though the Church—as our mother—is inviting us to view life through a more seasonal lens.

Yes, there are going to be seasons when you, as a parent, feel the burden of backbreaking, sleep-deprived, constant labor. It's thankless. It's to a large degree anonymous. It's necessary, but that doesn't make it any easier. It's in these moments that the devil draws near and whispers in your ear; he invites you—as he did with Adam and Eve—to turn your attention to self.

Just a few of the lies the devil especially likes to throw out to parents include the following:

No one notices.
But what about you?
No one understands.
Your partner isn't pulling their weight.
No one appreciates your sacrifices.
You're on your own.
God's not listening.
This is hopeless.
It will never change.

Have you harbored any of these ideas—consciously or unconsciously—during your day-to-day? If so, it doesn't make you horrible; it makes you *human*. In fact, if you're in the devil's crosshairs, it isn't necessarily that you're doing anything wrong but, rather, that you are likely doing things right! St. Angela Merici told us, "The devil doesn't sleep, but seeks the ruin of your soul in a thousand ways." Our first pope, St. Peter, too, warned that, "Your opponent the devil is prowling around like a roaring lion looking for [someone] to devour" (1 Pt 5:8).

If you stay focused on the mistakes you've made and your desire to change the past, you are not parenting. It's the past. Let it go. If you need to go to Confession, quit screwing around and go. Your kids need you to be present in the present. The only thing separating you and your children from sainthood . . . is you.

Sinners Raising Saints?

If Catholic history has taught us anything, it's that some of the worst sinners become the greatest saints. Think about it: There are souls right now—atheists and agnostics—who will become the greatest of modern saints. It's true. Your very own kids (far holier than most adults) could become saints. If you think that's unrealistic, the devil has already won in your home. It's time to claim that as a lie, rebuke it, and cast it out of your life.

If you truly want your children not only to breathe but to *live*, and not only to live but to *thrive* (Jn 10:10), then you, as parents, need to remember the goal. The great nineteenth-century French poet and novelist Léon Bloy said,

"There is only one tragedy in the end, not to have been a saint. The worst thing is not to commit crimes but, rather, not to accomplish the good that one could have done." Bloy lived a hard life, experiencing both poverty and immense personal suffering, but he did not lose his perspective. A convert, he found an invaluable context to suffering within the Catholic faith.

The only thing separating you and your children from sainthood . . . is you.

And he's not the only one. Consider these tortured and sinful souls we now hail as saints:

- St. Olga was a mass murderer before she heard the Gospel.

- St. Callixtus was an embezzler and cheat.

- St. Pelagia was promiscuous.

- St. Vladimir was a rapist and murderer.

- St. Genesius publicly and repeatedly mocked God.

- St. Margaret of Cortona was a mistress.

- St. Camillus de Lellis was a con man.

- St. Moses the Ethiopian was a violent gang leader.

- St. Ignatius of Loyola was a full-on narcissist.

- St. Augustine was drunken and promiscuous.

- St. Thomas Becket was a rich, self-involved hedonist and egotist.

- St. Philip Howard was a vain, entitled, elitist playboy, socialite, and gambler.

- St. Matthew was a cheating, despised tax collector.

- St. Mary of Egypt was a seductress and prostitute.

- St. Paul was a murderer of Christians.

- Bl. Bartolo Longo was a satanist "priest" before getting ordained a true priest.

- Ven. Matt Talbot was a raging and abusive alcoholic before his conversion.

The thing is, God's not afraid of our flaws or imperfections or sins.

All of these egregious sins, and yet we celebrate these men and women? God's mercy is real. It is limitless just as he is limitless. God's grace and mercy work *through* and *around* and *within* and *beyond* all of our misgivings and missed moments as parents, provided that we put our kids—his kids—in his divine path every chance we get. Just think, if the Father in heaven is so incredibly merciful as to put up with—and never give up on—the above list of sinners, how could he ever give up on you, even on your worst day of parenting? Our kids, like us, are inevitably going to make mistakes. They, like us, are flawed and imperfect. The thing is, God's not afraid of our flaws or imperfections or sins. He's not afraid to get into our muck and get his hands dirty. In fact, that's exactly what he wants to do!

Just Keep Chippin' Away at It

It confounded all of the great artistic minds of the day. For years, the mammoth block of marble was surveyed yet left untouched by every sculptor who examined it. Nearly four decades went by as the gorgeous marble slab sat unused, occupying space in the back lot of the cathedral in Florence. The problem, you ask? It wasn't the height, standing about eighteen feet tall, or the girth, weighing in at well over six tons. No, the problem was a hole running all the way through it, left by the last artist who'd attempted to sculpt the marble. None of the artists who followed could figure out how to work with such a profound imperfection.

It wasn't until 1501, when Michelangelo Buonarroti gazed upon the giant slab, that the marble would find its true purpose—to become his acclaimed statue of David. Michelangelo would slay the giant marble by forming from it the great giant-slayer.

Michelangelo perceived something that other minds— even brilliant, gifted minds—failed to see. He deduced that by tilting and turning the stone to a very precise angle, he could carve around the hole. In the hands of a master, the problem that rendered the marble seemingly useless became part of the solution in a masterpiece. Others saw flawed stone; Michelangelo saw the stone slinger. Some quote Michelangelo as saying, "I saw the angel in the marble and carved until I set him free."

You may look at your current situation—your marriage or family, job or debt, addiction or temptations, health or future—and see only the flaws. You might view a child or situation or even yourself as hopeless or impossible for God to change. If so, your vision of God is far too small. God can work with those "holes"; the master potter (Is 64:7) is also a master sculptor who can chisel away your rough edges if you let him. Michelangelo saw greatness in a flawed rock. Imagine how much more greatness the Father sees in us living stones!

Regardless of your personal situation or daily cross (Lk 9:23), prayer will alter and elevate your perspective. We all have hurdles in our lives that seem insurmountable. David had one named Goliath. Do you trust that the Lord is not only in the battle beside you but also fighting the battle *for you* (Ex 14:14)?

Thank God that he sees more in us than we see in ourselves! All God needs to make a saint out of you is your humility. All God needs to craft you into a parental masterpiece is your consent and humble prayer. If you cooperate with him, you'll probably become a saint . . . which could lead to a statue made in your image. How's that for irony?

Let our Father, the master sculptor, take the chisel and hone you, daily. Pray and ask the Holy Spirit to unleash God's greatness—a greatness that lies within you both as parents—to a world desperately in need of it. Then, and only then, can you ask the Lord to help you chisel away your own children's rough edges and help them to unearth their own greatness. Every strategy and insight we have offered in this book—the stories of failure, moments of grace, scripture verses, quotes, and practical ideas (as well as the prayer resources and couples' testimonials to follow)—relies for its effectiveness on your desire to get yourselves and your children, God's children, home to heaven.

If you want to move from a not-quite-holy family to a truly holy family, you need God's grace. And if you want to raise saints, become saints.

May God bless you always and in all ways.

Moving Forward (Practical Steps)

1. Read the following Bible passages and commit them to memory:

   The LORD will fight for you; you have only to keep still.
   —Exodus 14:14

   He saved us and called us to a holy life, not according to our works but according to his own design and the grace bestowed on us in Christ Jesus before time began. —2 Timothy 1:9

   We love because he first loved us. —1 John 4:19

2. With your spouse, make a list of challenging situations you've experienced in your relationship and talk or journal about how God was present within them. Pray about them as a couple and thank God for the stresses and learning experiences he has allowed in your life. The more present we are to how God has moved in our

own struggles, the more we can help our children when God wants to show them something positive within a perceived negative.

3. Read through the appendix of prayers, and commit to specific prayer times as a couple and family.

Closing Prayer

Lord, thank you for the gift of struggles in our parenthood. Thank you for all of those moments when you allow us to wonder about your divine plan and invite us to trust you more deeply. Thank you for the gift of permitting us to guide your children back to you. Forgive us for the many times we react reflexively rather than respond to your grace and perfect plan. Help us to have a higher perspective. Grant us wisdom, Lord. May we never forget that no matter how much we love these children you have given us, you love them perfectly and infinitely more. Amen.

Appendix 1

Prayers and Devotions for Couples and Families

Prayer to St. Michael the Archangel

St. Michael the Archangel,
defend us in battle.
Be our defense against the wickedness and snares
    of the devil.
May God rebuke him, we humbly pray,
and do thou,
O Prince of the heavenly hosts,
by the power of God,
thrust into hell Satan,
and all the evil spirits,
who prowl about the world
seeking the ruin of souls.
Amen.

Prayer of Abandonment

Father,
I abandon myself into your hands;

do with me what you will.
Whatever you may do, I thank you:
I am ready for all, I accept all.

Let only your will be done in me,
and in all your creatures—
I wish no more than this, O Lord.

Into your hands I commend my soul:
I offer it to you with all the love of my heart,
for I love you, Lord, and so need to give myself,
to surrender myself into your hands without reserve,
and with boundless confidence,
for you are my Father.
Amen.

—*Bl. Charles de Foucauld*

Consecration to the Holy Family

O Jesus, our most loving Redeemer, who having come to enlighten the world with thy teaching and example, didst will to pass the greater part of thy life in humility and subjection to Mary and Joseph in the poor home of Nazareth, thus sanctifying the Family that was to be an example for all Christian families, graciously receive our family as it dedicates and consecrates itself to thee this day. Do thou protect us, guard us, and establish amongst us thy holy fear, true peace, and concord in Christian love: in order that by living according to the divine pattern of thy family we may be able, all of us without exception, to attain to eternal happiness.

Mary, dear Mother of Jesus and Mother of us, by thy kindly intercession make this our humble offering acceptable in the sight of Jesus, and obtain for us his graces and blessings.

O St. Joseph, most holy Guardian of Jesus and Mary, help us by thy prayers in all our spiritual and temporal needs; that so we may be enabled to praise our divine Savior Jesus, together with Mary and thee, for all eternity.

(Recite the Our Father, Hail Mary, and Glory Be three times.)

Amen.

Prayer for Our Family from St. Teresa of Calcutta

Heavenly Father,
you have given us the model of life
in the Holy Family of Nazareth.
Help us, O Loving Father,
to make our family another Nazareth
where love, peace, and joy reign.
May it be deeply contemplative,
intensely eucharistic,
revived with joy.

Help us to stay together in joy
and sorrow in family prayer.
Teach us to see Jesus in the members of our families,
especially in their distressing disguise.
May the eucharistic heart of Jesus
make our hearts humble like his
and help us to carry out our family duties

in a holy way.
May we love one another
as God loves each one of us,
more and more each day,
and forgive each other's faults
as you forgive our sins.
Help us, O Loving Father,
to take whatever you give
and give whatever you take with a big smile.

Immaculate Heart of Mary,
cause of our joy, pray for us.

St. Joseph, pray for us.

Holy Guardian Angels,
be always with us,
guide and protect us.
Amen.

Prayer for Fathers from St. John XXIII

St. Joseph, guardian of Jesus and chaste husband of Mary, you passed your life in loving fulfillment of duty. You supported the holy family of Nazareth with the work of your hands. Kindly protect those who trustingly come to you. You know their aspirations, their hardships, their hopes. They look to you because they know you will understand and protect them. You too knew trial, labor, and weariness. But amid the worries of material life, your soul was full of deep peace and sang out in true joy through intimacy with God's Son entrusted to you and with Mary, his tender Mother. Assure those you protect that they do not labor alone. Teach them to find Jesus near them and to watch over him faithfully as you have done. Amen.

Litany of Humility

O Jesus, meek and humble of heart,
Hear me.
From the desire of being esteemed,
Deliver me, O Jesus.
From the desire of being loved,
Deliver me, O Jesus.
From the desire of being extolled,
Deliver me, O Jesus.
From the desire of being honored,
Deliver me, O Jesus.
From the desire of being praised,
Deliver me, O Jesus.
From the desire of being preferred to others,
Deliver me, O Jesus.
From the desire of being consulted,
Deliver me, O Jesus.
From the desire of being approved,
Deliver me, O Jesus.
From the fear of being humiliated,
Deliver me, O Jesus.
From the fear of being despised,
Deliver me, O Jesus.
From the fear of suffering rebukes,
Deliver me, O Jesus.
From the fear of being calumniated,

Deliver me, O Jesus.
From the fear of being forgotten,
Deliver me, O Jesus.
From the fear of being ridiculed,
Deliver me, O Jesus.
From the fear of being wronged,
Deliver me, O Jesus.
From the fear of being suspected,
Deliver me, O Jesus.

That others may be loved more than I,
Jesus, grant me the grace to desire it.
That others may be esteemed more than I,
Jesus, grant me the grace to desire it.
That, in the opinion of the world, others may increase
    and I may decrease,
Jesus, grant me the grace to desire it.
That others may be chosen and I set aside,
Jesus, grant me the grace to desire it.
That others may be praised and I go unnoticed,
Jesus, grant me the grace to desire it.
That others may be preferred to me in everything,
Jesus, grant me the grace to desire it.
That others may become holier than I, provided that I
    may become as holy as I should,
Jesus, grant me the grace to desire it.
Amen.

Chaplet of Divine Mercy

Begin with the Sign of the Cross, one Our Father, one Hail Mary, and the Apostles' Creed.

Then, on the Our Father beads say the following:

Eternal Father, I offer you the Body and Blood, Soul and Divinity of your dearly beloved Son, our Lord Jesus Christ, in atonement for our sins and those of the whole world.

On the ten Hail Mary beads say the following:

For the sake of his sorrowful Passion, have mercy on us and on the whole world.

Repeat for all five decades.

Conclude with (three times):

Holy God, Holy Mighty One, Holy Immortal One, have mercy on us and on the whole world.

Appendix 2

Testimonials from Some Amazing Catholic Couples

Empowered, Not Perfect: Raising Children Who Can Make Mistakes | The Baniewicz Family

"You parent differently now than you did with me. That's all I'm saying," stated our oldest daughter after a short visit home during college. We responded with a resounding, "Yes, we do parent differently! We are older, a little more tired, and have learned some things along the way." It's true. We have parented our younger children differently than the oldest of our five. That's because we are always learning and, to be honest, we didn't really know what we were doing when we started (not that we have it all figured out now).

When our first child was born, we were convinced that she was the most brilliant, advanced, beautiful, holy child in the whole world. We didn't want anyone telling us how to raise her, because, you know, we were in our mid twenties and had it all figured out. We had worked with youth for many years, so we thought we already had a good handle on how to do this. We discussed with each other what we liked and didn't like about the job our parents did with us. We knew we could do it better. Except we didn't.

I (Phil) remember vividly a religious sister sitting with us at dinner during a training conference. My daughter was being adorable as usual, but she made a comment that, let's just say, wasn't very adorable. I was shocked and a little embarrassed, so I bent down to talk quietly with her and expressed my displeasure at what she had said. She immediately became deflated. As I look back, I know I embarrassed her in front of others. The sister watched the situation play out in front of her, and although I don't think she could hear what I said, she made a comment to me when my wife took our daughter to the bathroom. "Oh, don't crush her spirit. She is such a wonderful little girl." It hit me. I had thought that if my daughter wasn't perfect, that was a poor reflection on us as parents. And what I also began learning was that *if I transferred my own issues of trying to be perfect to her, it would eventually impact her negatively as she grew.* We needed help. There were three things we did:

First, we signed up for parenting classes. Now, to my wife Lisa's credit, she was always reading and learning about how to parent. I was the one who was too insecure to admit I needed help. Well, now I had reached the tipping point. We went through a sixteen-week, Christian-based class that was offered in our parish. It was a true godsend. It was so helpful that, as the years have passed, we continue to go to classes or watch videos to help us parent better. And we still use tools we learned from the first class in raising our children.

Second, we stopped worrying about our kids not being perfect, or anyone's perception of us as not being good parents. Instead, we learned to relax a little more as our children made mistakes, spoke out of turn, or made bad decisions. All of us make mistakes as we navigate this journey to heaven. We began making an effort to keep our eyes on their future, helping them become the person God created them to be as we teach them, give them a firm foundation, and point them toward Jesus. Most of all, we made sure that they knew we loved them and God loved them. We still expected them to be good, do their best, and be kind to others, but we became more comfortable with allowing them to make mistakes, fail, be foolish at times, and just enjoy the present moment. Heck, we are all beautiful messes who are incredibly loved by the Almighty God. What a gift!

Third, we changed how we raise our kids. We don't expect perfection, nor do we take it personally if our kids aren't the best at something. They are all such precious gifts from the Lord, and it is our responsibility to help them grow each day. Laughter fills our home more and more every day. The kids (like us) still make mistakes. Yet we help them journey through both successes and failures. We realize each of our children is a different, yet precious gift. Thank God we have learned to adapt and try to parent more effectively with each child.

Allowing the "Small Things" to Remain Small: Dismissing the Argument | The Fitzgerald Family

One of the best things that we have done in our twenty-four years of marriage is to stop fighting. Too bad it took us twenty-two years to figure out how to do that. And truth be told, time did not have very much to do with it.

For the first twenty-two years of our marriage, communication and discussions were, for the most part, pretty typical for a married couple raising several children. With four children and a stay-at-home mom, we were a one-income family. And with the winning lottery ticket always about four numbers out of reach, our finances put a significant amount of stress on us. Job changes—some voluntary, some not—helped increase the stress, along with many other issues that face most couples trying to raise a family these days. All this added up to fairly frequent bickering, the occasional escalating fight, and every once in a while the "we haven't talked in three days" blowout.

So what changed? In the summer of 2017, right at the twenty-two-year mark of our marriage, Erin was diagnosed with an aggressive form of breast cancer. We consulted with our primary-care physician, a surgeon, an oncologist, and a radiologist. We talked, we discerned, and we prayed. Erin ultimately decided to take the most drastic options of treatment available because those would give her the highest probability that this cancer would never return. She wanted to do everything in her power to ensure that she would be around for our children as long as possible. If the cancer was to return at some point in the future, she would have peace of mind knowing that she had done all she could and that this was God's will. Treatment began with a bilateral mastectomy, followed by three months of intensive chemotherapy and another nine months of visits to the oncologist for more infusions of medication. And the past two summers have included follow-up surgeries.

So how did that cancer diagnosis affect our communication and bring us to a point where we don't fight anymore? To be honest, we are not quite sure. In fact, for a long time we didn't realize it. And then when we did, we didn't want to talk about it—we didn't want to spoil the new track record of no fighting. Eventually we started to discuss it, and here's what we are learning.

Erin's battle with cancer forced her to a level of vulnerability that she had never known before. She is a strong person and, like many of us, struggled with letting her guard down. In the past, in our discussions Erin normally became combative. She was well equipped to hold her ground and could spar pretty well with me (Sean). But during those first few months after surgery, she had to rely on me more than ever. By the grace of God, I was able to serve at her bedside in a way that left her appreciative and grateful in a way that is not easily forgotten.

For me, it's pretty simple. My wife looked cancer in the face and never blinked. Of course she shed some tears, but not many. And a breakdown never happened. Our strength came from God's grace, poured out upon us through the sacrament of our marriage and the sacramental life we strive to live, staying close to the Eucharist and Confession.

And no doubt the prayers offered up by friends and family have sustained us. Our battle with cancer has left us with an entirely new level of respect, admiration, and appreciation for each other. When you've been on the front line of a battle with someone and you've stood a step or two behind while they led the charge, the last thing you want to do is to bring strife or battle back into their life. I won't be the catalyst for argument in my wife's daily living.

And of course there's the perspective we have gained, which is so common in these scenarios that it's practically cliché: When you're faced with your own mortality or the mortality of someone you love, it truly does help you weed out the small stuff and treat it as such. So many arguments in marriage start with the small things, and because of the daily stress and our own pride they quickly escalate into something more. My wife and I now simply refuse to allow that to happen. These days we rarely get past a few words of disagreement before one of us makes a joke that derails the argument or simply and humbly tries to see the other person's perspective.

Of course, with the arguing gone, we have drawn closer, and we have certainly lowered the level of discontent and stress in our family. While we wish it hadn't taken twenty-two years and cancer to get us to this point, we are so grateful that we are here.

If you love someone, set them free . . . from arguing with you. It's usually not worth it. You usually don't mean it, and when we humble ourselves, it makes way for more of God's grace to get in. Which is what we need the most.

A House Built on Rock: How the Sacrament of Marriage Supports Us in Times of Difficulty | The Griffith Family

Recently we had the honor of going to a Catholic wedding for a wonderful friend from Mexico. For those of you who have not experienced the reception traditions of this country, there are a number of special and symbolic activities that are both joyful and deeply meaningful. One such tradition is called *La Vibora de la Mar,* or The Serpent of the Sea. Think conga line meets London Bridges.

The bride and groom stand on chairs a short distance apart, holding either end of the bridal veil. A select few bridesmaids and groomsmen surround the bride and groom while the wedding guests form a train and dance in line, snaking around the dance floor faster and faster to the increasing tempo of the music. All the while, the line gets closer and closer to the bride and groom until they're bumping into each other. It gets chaotic and can be quite exhilarating and physical, especially for the groom, as the couple are buffeted by the moving storm of people surrounding them. Their attendants surrounding the chairs protect them or catch them should they fall.

In broken Spanish, I (Tony) inquired of an elderly guest as to the meaning of this custom. It was explained that this ritual symbolizes the strength of the bond between the husband and wife amid the challenges and trials that will come, with their friends there to protect and support them. It was a splendid visual analogy of living into the sacramental bond of love in the midst of the overwhelming stresses and challenges that occasionally occur, as well as the communal nature of our love within the Body of Christ.

In our twenty-eight years of marriage, we have faced a time of potentially marriage-threatening difficulties. Feeling discouraged in our parenting and disconnected in our marriage in a time of great stress knocked us off our center. Thankfully we have had the opportunity to learn from that experience. We know that *the joy and blessing of living this beautiful sacramental life will inevitably involve times of challenge, and we know that the foundation of our faith is that house built on solid rock that helps us through.* But how exactly?

Some practical advice here is helpful in terms of what we learned to bring us back into that life of love that God wants for each of us.

First, communication between us and in our prayer lives was that primary foundation upon which everything else rested. Our darkest of times brought us to our knees together, which was reason enough for God to allow us to undergo this experience.

Second, we openly discussed our situation with family and Catholic couple friends whose relationships we respected. They refocused us on the fact that the best thing we could do for our kids was to have a strong marriage and to make the marital relationship, not our kids, the first priority. Our relationship as husband and wife needed to come first.

Third, we sought faith-focused professionals. Whether they were parent coaches, counselors, psychiatrists, or psychologists, faith-focused professionals were instrumental in giving us tools and ideas that we still rely on to this day. The strategies these professionals taught us continue to be immensely helpful in ongoing times of stress and uncertainty.

Fourth, as suggested by a counselor, we resumed those positive activities that were our God-given passions. For Carol it was as simple as returning to women's tennis each week. For Tony, that involved going back to playing the drums in our church band and starting back with his men's Bible study. We also continued our date nights and recommitted to our monthly Catholic couples group called "Teams of Our Lady."

So when the Serpent of the Sea tries to drown your joy, keep these lessons in mind. Dive into your relationship with God and each other, stay afloat with the help of family and friends, chart a new course with direction from professionals, and tack back to those positive, life-affirming pursuits that God has called you to from the beginning. These strategies worked for us in getting our heads back above water and returning to a life of passion and purpose, leaning into the beautiful, loving, and joy-filled Sacrament of Marriage.

Loving Them to God's Arms: He Is Bigger Than Our Worst Parenting | The Hickman Family

We were nearly asleep after a long day when I (Cana) suddenly became aware of a screen glowing from underneath the door of our fifteen-year-old's room across the hall. *Is he on his phone right now?* I wondered, irate and fearful. He knew the rules, knew the dangers of the internet, and struggled with prudent internet usage. Not only was he in trouble, but his behavior hit me hard. *I'm such a terrible mother. Why do we even have screens in this house anyway?* I thought.

As I sat there in a guilt-ridden daze, my husband, Ennie, jumped out of bed to address the situation. My heart pounded in my chest as he confirmed my fears. Our son in fact was on the internet in his room after hours. We had failed.

After a scolding and a confiscation of the device, both of which were highly reactionary, Ennie and I headed back to bed—all three of us quite shaken up. We lay down not even knowing how to pray and just kept saying, "Lord have mercy!" over and over again. We felt like we could hear our son's sobs, too. After a few minutes, we heard the back door open. I sprang out of bed only to see my son—my precious, beautiful, intelligent, creative, funny, heart-of-gold, goofball son—riding his bike away into the very dark night just as it began to rain, hard. (When it comes to the Hickmans, God really does have a flair for the dramatic.) I called his name, but he didn't even look back. He was filled with guilt and shame, and he was running.

Not only had we blown it as far as keeping him safe online but now we'd blown it by not keeping him in our love. He was running away! I was a total wreck. Heart still pounding and ears ringing, I jumped in Ennie's truck to follow him. He'd gotten enough of a head start and it was raining so hard that I couldn't see him, but he had headed in the direction of my in-laws' neighborhood, so I went that way. After a couple of blocks, I suddenly knew where he was going. Sure enough, as I pulled into the parking lot of our perpetual adoration chapel, I saw his bike parked just outside the door. It was a sacred moment for me.

Walking into that chapel, I saw my son's head bowed low in humility, in reverence, in repentance, and in prayer, and I recognized that the same infinite God who has so relentlessly pursued my heart for forty years and loves me in all my brokenness is also pursuing my son. Such comfort it gave to my mother's heart to see where my son fled in his moment of need. He ran to the arms of Christ and was comforted. There he received the divine mercy that we, his earthly parents, couldn't demonstrate.

As that beautiful monstrance shone its light down upon my son and I sat in the chapel that evening, I wept. I wept because I saw my son hurting. I wept in agony knowing that my children are probably going to have to fight the same battles I've had to fight. I wept because God's grace is real and his consolation was touching both my son and me. After some time, he got up to leave and we embraced.

We loaded up his bike and drove back home. When we walked in the door, there was his dad, waiting for him with hot chocolate in hand. Mercy. Forgiveness. God is making us all better.

As parents, we desire to instill in our children the knowledge that they've been chosen by God and that, no matter what, he will never abandon them. Somehow, even in the midst of our "bad parenting," God revealed his love to our son that night. *The truth is, God is bigger than our best parenting, and he's also bigger than our worst parenting.* Our job is to let go and love our kids into the Father's arms. The temptation is to beat ourselves up for the many ways we fail them—the many times we make promises we can't keep, and all the impatient, undisciplined, selfish interactions we have with our children. But, if we do our best to love them with the Father's love, point them to the sacraments, and demonstrate our own need for relationship with Christ every day, God's grace can take it from there. He is drawing them to himself.

Parents, it's simply not up to you. We'll repeat that because it's important. It's not up to you, because, ultimately, they are his. Letting go and giving yourself permission to be less than perfect might be the hardest thing you ever have to do as a parent. But in doing so, you give God permission to work miracles.

The Lord Is Near: Recognizing and Eliminating Anxiety in Our Family | The Morgan Family

We chose Philippians 4:4–9 as our second reading at our wedding. If you've never read it, we strongly encourage you to open your family Bible and give it a prayerful review. Beautifully, the message is more important and vital for us today than it was twenty years ago.

We are both type A personalities and overly busy. Phrases like "have no anxiety at all" and "the Lord is near" are generally not in our vocabulary. More often, we are overwhelmed and stressed, and sometimes we're disconnected with each other and our children. To eliminate that disconnection, we have two strategies: First, in our home, and with each other, there is absolutely no interrupting, teasing, making fun of, sarcasm, or bullying. Second, we eat dinner together as a family at least two to three times per week.

We admit that these strategies appear to be basic and simple, but they're actually harder to implement than we expected. We came up with the first strategy when our third child developed a stutter. The speech therapist told us that the stutter was likely caused by family interaction, specifically our behavior of interrupting one another. Possibly, our child involuntarily developed a stutter so that he could continue to "speak" through his pauses between sentences, without interruption. The therapist told us we needed to stop interrupting one another. She was direct and blunt.

That night, we shared the news with our family that we could no longer interrupt one another. Our second-born was immediately indignant and said something to the effect of, "Hey, wait, you mean I can't speak when someone else is speaking? That stinks, and I don't like it! I won't change!" We had to work with her, our other children, and each other to ensure that we didn't interrupt. It was hard. We had to commit to this decision over and over and again and again. It took discipline and a conscious choice of kindness and patience. Amazingly, four years later, our child no longer stutters. The speech therapist was shocked because stuttering is almost always an established pattern for life. We believe he no longer stutters because he knows that when he speaks within our family, he is heard. He is connected with the whole family.

In addition to the no-interruption rule, we do not tease or bully one another. We aren't sarcastic with one another. We don't make fun of one another. Rather, we ensure that the joy and laughter in our home never come at another's expense. It's a conscious choice that we enforce. We even created a rule; it's from Michael Corleone: "Never go against the family." When we see our children or each other teasing, we know that we are not following our rule, and our home is not a house of peace. We immediately stop, we hug (and require the kids to hug one another), we apologize, and we move on. We try to be kind the next time.

The second strategy of having family meals together was easier to implement when the children were younger. Now that our children are in sports and other activities and have tremendous study requirements, the time for family dinner can easily fall away. However, we make a conscious decision to eat meals together as often as possible, and at least two to three times per week. During our family meals, there's no phone, no TV, no iPad. It's just us, and we talk. We require everyone to participate. You can't sit at our table and be quiet. We use the time to learn about our children and each other. During our meals, we love on one another and connect.

We believe that these two strategies allow to us to eliminate anxiety and recognize that the Lord is near. Through these strategies, we attempt to pursue the true, the honorable, the just, the pure, the lovely, the gracious, and the praiseworthy. Then, during these times, the God of peace is with us.

We wish you all of God's blessings on your journey.

Mark and Melanie Hart minister to married and engaged couples in group and personal settings. Mark is the chief information officer and executive vice president of Life Teen International. He is an award-winning producer of Bible study DVDs and the author of more than twenty books, including the best-selling and award-winning *Blessed Are the Bored in Spirit*. Melanie spends her free time ministering to, counseling, and mentoring women of all ages. The Harts are coauthors of *Embracing God's Plan for Marriage: A Bible Study for Couples* and *Getting More Out of Marriage*.

A graduate of the University of Notre Dame, Mark is a blogger, podcaster, and international speaker. He is a research fellow at the St. Paul Center for Biblical Theology.

The couple lives in the Phoenix, Arizona, area with their four children.

Biblegeek.com
Facebook: @MarkHart99
Twitter: @LT_thebiblegeek
Instagram: @biblegeek

AVE

AVE MARIA PRESS

Founded in 1865, Ave Maria Press,
a ministry of the Congregation of
Holy Cross, is a Catholic publishing
company that serves the spiritual and
formative needs of the Church and its
schools, institutions, and ministers;
Christian individuals and families; and
others seeking spiritual nourishment.

For a complete listing of titles from

Ave Maria Press

Sorin Books

Forest of Peace

Christian Classics

visit www.avemariapress.com

AVE | AVE MARIA PRESS
      | Notre Dame, IN
A Ministry of the United States Province of Holy Cross